AF443385

THE FLOWERS WHITBREAD

Rugby World '96

THE FLOWERS WHITBREAD Rugby World '96

NIGEL STARMER-SMITH
AND IAN ROBERTSON

Queen Anne Press

A QUEEN ANNE PRESS BOOK

© Lennard Associates Ltd 1995

First published in 1995 by
Queen Anne Press, a division of
Lennard Associates Ltd
Mackerye End
Harpenden, Herts AL5 5DR

All rights reserved. No part of this publication may be reproduced,
stored in a retrieval system, or transmitted, in any form or by any
means, without the prior permission in writing of the publisher, nor
be otherwise circulated in any form of binding or cover other than
that in which it is published without a similar condition including
this condition being imposed on the subsequent purchaser.

A catalogue entry is available from the British Library

ISBN 1 85291 566 8

Editor: Caroline North
Production Editor: Chris Hawkes
Reproduction by Leaside Graphics
Printed and bound in England by
William Caple & Co. Ltd

The publishers and editors would like to thank Colin Elsey of Colorsport for
providing most of the photographs for this book.

Thanks for additional photographs to David Gibson of Fotosport, RFU
and Sportsfile.

Thanks also to Whitbread for their continuing support and to Cathay Pacific,
The Hongkong Bank and Save and Prosper for their contributions
to this year's edition.

CONTENTS

COMMENT
One Flew Over the Cuckoo's Nest (Tony Hallett) 6
'Si Monumentum Requiris, Circumspice' (Dudley Wood) 8
England's Representative Muddle (Paul Stephens) 13
THE RUGBY WORLD CUP 1995
Wales in the World Cup and Beyond (David Parry-Jones) 18
Themba's T-Shirt and Other Tales (John Inverdale) 22
A Magnificent Rugby Occasion (Clem Thomas) 26
Burto's Bashers XV (Mike Burton) 32
ON THE HOME FRONT
Gavin Hastings – Leading From the Front (Bill McLaren) 36
England's Dilemma (Paul Ackford) 39
RUGBY WORLDWIDE
The Tours (Bill Mitchell) 44
Refereeing the Modern Game (Ed Morrison) 49
The Next Logical Step: A European Club Superleague? (Chris Thau) .. 52
The Bledisloe Cup Centenary (Clem Thomas) 57
LOOKING BACK
Rugby's First Merit Table? (Peter Watson) 62
25 Years Ago (Nigel Starmer-Smith) 67
A World Cup Quiz (Nigel Starmer-Smith) 80
REVIEW OF THE SEASON 1994-5
The Five Nations Championship (Bill McLaren) 83
Key Players for 1995-6 (Ian Robertson) 89
Club Scene (Bill Mitchell, Sean Diffley, Norman Mair,
David Stewart, Chris Thau) 94
The Whitbread Flowers/*Rugby World* Awards 115
A Summary of the Season (Bill Mitchell) 116
FIXTURES 1995-6 (Bill Mitchell) 124

One Flew Over the Cuckoo's Nest

by Tony Hallett, Secretary of the RFU

Tony Hallett.

The train wound its way up from Cape Town through the mountains and into the Little Karoo. A final, dramatic, defiant burst of setting sun and peaceful darkness descended upon the vast land of South Africa. Time then for reflection and also for the writing of this introduction to the new rugby season. There is no better place to write it than from the southern hemisphere, where jointly rugby politics and money beat an almost incessant tattoo. The game shouldn't be so dominated, but in reality these matters will take the headlines while rugby goes through its own metamorphosis. This season heralds the watershed in the affairs of a sport so often inaccurately described as an amateur game played for recreation and fun. Of course, for a substantial majority the game is and will always be a recreation in which the individual's net cash situation will be a cheerful voluntary loss. But it is not so at international level now, and certainly it is here that great change is imminent.

It is an opportunity, then, for the members of the International Board to cast aside the shadowlands of professional interpretation; to renounce the word amateurism as being the singular principle upon which the game is founded. It is, after all, an insult to our and indeed all rugby peoples' intelligence to suggest that the game is amateur. Just look in the car park at any international training session and see those top-of-the-range limousines, hear the talk, see the stars – these are not the lot of the amateur. Since few begrudge the international players and the many aspirants the opportunity to gain from their singular dedication and time commitment, it is clear that the 'amateur' regulations require rapid and incisive surgery. This introduction was written before the International Board meeting in August 1995 at which we shall be able to judge for ourselves how sharp is the surgeon's knife. The opportunity is there, the hour beckons and, lest there be any of uncertain mind, perhaps some words borrowed from Churchill might encourage: 'Administrators ride around on tigers they dare not dismount and the tigers are getting hungry.'

Enough of the great debate; whatever the outcome, it will surely run a while yet. There is much discussion about expanding our club competitiveness into Europe, or even further afield, and there is a lot of sense in the idea. There is a feeling of urgency about the plans, but there shouldn't be panic. To underwrite a successful competition, space must be found in this already cluttered and overplayed season. What may suit clubs from Wales might not suit the French or the English. The pressure on players will increase too – and a trade-off commitment to divisional/club rugby and country will be necessary. I would hope to see a viable and exciting new competition in place for season 1996–7. It may come earlier for some countries, but it would be better if it kicked off with all the runners and riders in the stalls.

The southern hemisphere's £360 million News International philosophy and revamped provincial and 'Three Nations Championship' is significant and lays down a clear challenge to the competitiveness and financial infrastructure of the northern hemisphere. It isn't a case, though, of getting mean, but more one of getting even. We must look ever more to our competitiveness and playing standards; certainly we must strive to sustain our fixtures with our friends Down Under and never let them out of our sights. We must seek comparable financial support without the strings that could form a noose. Talk of their playing on a different financial playing field from ours and hints of isolationism are just illusions. In any case, that is what the International Board is appointed to sort out.

One final thing, and you might expect this from me. Twickenham completes this autumn – a 75,000-capacity all-seater stadium built to the highest and sometimes expensive standards of safety and spectator support. Everyone and certainly every country has their own particular pride and joy, but if you are English you can let your heart swell a little. It is £70 million good and has enough bars, brasseries, cafés, restaurants – and the loos to support their indulgence – than any other rugby stadium in the world.

Now, where is that cuckoo's nest?

P.S. Not a word above, written before the IB Paris 'Summit', has been changed. We must now march positively into rugby's new Millenium with a code of conduct that underpins professional Rugby Union. In so doing, we must hold fast to that which is honourable and of good report in the 'old game', seek the best for the new and stick together.

'Si Monumentum Requiris, Circumspice'

BY DUDLEY WOOD, SECRETARY OF THE RFU 1986–95

Dudley Wood.

I feel as though I have been in rugby all my life – as a player, selector, team secretary, liaison officer, county secretary, county president and general factotum – just happy to be involved. 'Shorty', otherwise known as Graham Short, a permanent fixture as baggage master to incoming touring teams, never tires of recounting how he and the RFU secretary-to-be lugged two full sets of wet All Black jerseys to the launderette because the hotel laundry could not cope with them on the timescale required. Between us, 'we counted them all out and we counted them all back in'!

For as long as I can remember, whenever rugby football was discussed, some well-meaning original thinker would say, 'The game is at a crossroads,' an unmemorable expression at best, but certainly not true today. The crossroads are all behind us and it seems there is no turning back. Fortunately, I have not been asked to write about where the game is going, a task I would have declined, but where it has been in the last nine years.

In the 115 years from when the Rugby Football Union was formed up to my appointment in 1986, there had been 12 secretaries: numbers one to six were honorary holders of the office, the first paid appointment being in 1904. Even at that time, I have no doubt that there was plenty to keep a secretary occupied, with international matches to arrange, a County Championship to organise, committees to service and, shortly after that, a new ground to look after – but much more was to come.

Percy Coles, the first paid secretary, lasted only three years before he emigrated to Canada to become a fruit farmer, a course of action which was to commend itself to me any number of times during my term of office. I took over from the inestimable Air Commodore Bob Weighill, a good friend, in July 1986 after a short hand-over period. I was not new to the ways of the Rugby Union, having served on the committee as one of Surrey's representatives for the preceding five years, but I had scarcely if ever set foot in the offices at Twickenham and I did not know the staff. However, I inherited as my administrative secretary the redoubtable Dennis

Morgan, an ex-marine colonel, a strict disciplinarian with a heart of pure gold, and he soon taught me the form.

It was an interesting scenario at that time. Historically, the RFU had not been a particularly pro-active organisation. It had no real reason to be, responding as it did to the fairly undemanding requirements of its member counties and clubs and meeting its international obligations through the Five Nations committee and the International Board, on which the RFU had a strong if not dominant influence.

But to me, coming in from outside, and from a business background, there seemed to be both a mood and enormous scope for change. At Twickenham we needed to prepare for it, without relaxing the high standards of administration set by Bob Weighill and Dennis Morgan. The RFU offices were ex-directory and contact with the media and the outside world was either reactive or made through the medium of press releases. There was considerable mystique in many of our activities, not least the ticketing operation for international matches, whereby applications were handwritten in large ledgers. Our income was relatively modest, despite growing public interest and support, and opportunities were not being fully exploited.

We embarked tentatively on the process of change. Monthly press conferences were established with fairly flexible agenda to cater for matters of moment; a larger telephone switchboard, open to all, was installed and we began to think about computers. After a few months, I recall Dennis Morgan coming to see me and saying, 'I know I am not good at change, and I have to say that I don't like some of the things you are doing, but I want you to know that you have my total support.' I took that as a vote of confidence and I was very sad when he reached retirement age and departed a year or so later.

Opening up the union's activities to public scrutiny and particularly to that of the rugby writers is a double-edged weapon and we found that we had to be prepared to defend some fairly contentious policies from time to time, but on the whole the conferences, under Sir Peter Yarranton's astute chairmanship, worked well and led the way for other unions and even other sports.

The 1986–7 Five Nations Championship, my first as secretary, was disastrous for England. The opening match against Scotland, which was to be the only one we won, was postponed due to the frozen weather, which made it impossible for spectators – and indeed the Scottish team – to travel, and following the Wales game in Cardiff four England players, including the captain, were omitted from selection for the next match because of an outbreak of fighting. The inaugural World Cup that summer in Australia was to prove an even greater disaster for England.

Rightly or wrongly, huge store is set in every sport on the performance of the national team, and England were underperforming. No doubt this unhappy season helped to act as a catalyst, but huge changes of structure and organisation were on their way. Our coaching programmes had long been held up as models of good practice, but we did not have the structure needed to give players a competitive edge or even to bring the best players to the top. Turning from the top of the game to the bottom, there was increasing concern at the effect on schools rugby of teacher disputes and the decline in the playing of team games, which was bound to erode our recruitment base. This problem is now being addressed at a high level but the RFU felt it had to take some action independently.

Anyone for champagne? The England players mark their third Grand Slam in five years after beating Scotland in 1995.

The years that followed the disappointments of 1987 saw the revival of the Divisional Championship – not universally popular, but playing an important role at that time – the introduction of a comprehensive league structure embracing more than 1,200 clubs and the putting in place of the necessary 'stepping-stones' to England selection. None of this happened overnight and it demanded a huge commitment in committee time and resourcefulness. Consultation had to take place and major sponsorships had to be negotiated for the Divisional and County Championships, the club Leagues and also the knock-out Cup following the parting of the ways with

John Player. Although I liked the individuals with whom we dealt, I had never been comfortable with tobacco sponsorship.

The outcome of all this is there in the record books. Since that time, England have enjoyed considerable success at all levels but the highlights have been three Grand Slams, second and fourth places in successive World Cups and victory in the World Cup Sevens. Losing matches does not bother me greatly, even losing matches we should have won. There are two teams on the pitch and one of them generally has to lose. I think no worse of them for that. The important thing is that England, given their strength in numbers and their long tradition, should have the capability of competing with the best and the playing structure should be designed to achieve that. The transformation must be put down to many diverse factors which include the efforts of the players, Twickenham's technical staff, the team management and the committee, but transformation it was.

In the youth area, the RFU devised and implemented a youth development programme costing today in the region of £2 million per annum and involving the employment of a manager, four divisionally based technical administrators and some 42 youth development officers across the country, working with schools, clubs and counties. It has been widely praised as one of the best schemes in sport and we now have more mini-rugby, more clubs and more schools in membership than ever before in our history. A knock-out Cup for the 512 most junior clubs in membership has been added, with a final at Twickenham, and this has proved hugely popular.

The RFU acquired and developed as its Centre for Schools and Youth Rugby a fine ground at Castlecroft near Wolverhampton, the only union in the world to have such a facility. Nearly 60 games were played on that ground last season alone. The RFU are also part owners of the adjoining hotel where the youngsters are accommodated for their weekend courses and matches. Perhaps Castlecroft is the magic ingredient which has enabled England Schools to complete their second consecutive Grand Slam.

The great headquarters of rugby itself, Twickenham, has been rebuilt, and to a very high standard, to accommodate 75,000 seated spectators at a cost of some £70 million, none of it from outside sources. It is the largest and best-equipped rugby stadium in the world and on its completion, which is imminent, it will provide all the facilities one could wish for in terms of bars, restaurants, shops, museum, corporate hospitality, comfort and safety. Provision for the disabled in wheelchairs is the best of any major stadium in this country.

The RFU has always been mindful of its obligations to the less fortunate and a great deal of money has been raised for charitable causes over the years. Perhaps the best example was the RFU's initiative in organising the match between the Home Unions and the Rest of Europe played at Twickenham on Sunday 22 April 1990, which raised £300,000 for the Help Romania charity following the revolution in that country. The equivalent of a pound for every match ticket sold is now donated to the SPIRE fund for rugby's seriously injured and the target of £1 million will soon be achieved.

Relations with the local authority and local residents are now of a high order and the local schools sports day for which Twickenham is made available each summer without charge is always a happy event.

The credit for all the change that has taken place in recent years belongs to the RFU committee, supported by the Twickenham 'team'. It is of course fashionable to denigrate amateur committees and to accuse them of being involved out of self-interest or for the perks of the job. I have no doubt that there are administrators in the game to whom that would apply, but they are few and far between. Rugby is run by ex-players who want to maintain their involvement in the game and the friendships they have formed over the years, a system which has a long amateur tradition. All members of the RFU committee are subject to annual election or re-election by member clubs and this in itself is a mark of distinction. If they have been cast as unwilling to accept change, perhaps the foregoing recital will help to restore the balance. *Si monumentum requiris, circumspice.*

Twickenham's new West Stand, which takes the ground's capacity to 75,000.

England's Representative Muddle

BY PAUL STEPHENS

Those who took the trouble to watch Canterbury during their nine-match tour to England and Wales in November 1994 could hardly have failed to be impressed by the quality of the New Zealanders' rugby, or by the sheer pointlessness of their journey from the other side of the world, which hardly justified the air fare.

The players they faced are unlikely ever to forget it. It very soon became clear to the tourists that they were hopelessly undermatched. The club sides they met were in a state of collective trauma well before the penultimate game, against Bristol – the only team to provide the South Islanders with meaningful opposition. But by then, the squad, which contained All Blacks Richard Loe, Mike Brewer and the hugely promising outside-half Andrew Mehrtens, were bored with playing second-rate sides and wanted to get home as soon as they were able. Little, it seems, had been learned from the vain visit of Auckland the previous winter.

It was a perfect illustration of the mess England have created for themselves in the matter of representative rugby. Much of the confusion is the fault of the archaically named constituent bodies. This group, which comprises the 26 counties, the armed services and the universities, provides the nucleus of the Rugby Football Union's gigantic general committee. Now that Twickenham has wisely elected to operate with a less wieldy structure and a smaller executive, a great deal of their power and influence has diminished as far as the senior England teams are concerned. Within the vast commercial business that the international game has become, they are left to administer rugby at a much lower level.

On the afternoon when England were humiliating a depressingly weak Romania by 54–3, I was at

Andrew Mehrtens, the talented New Zealand fly-half, playing for Canterbury during a Ranfurly Shield game. Canterbury's tour to England was deemed by many to be pointless, as few sides posed them any problems.

"

Brierton Lane watching Canterbury extend the unrelenting trail of destruction on which they had embarked since arriving at Heathrow. In teeming rain they demolished West Hartlepool, scoring nine tries in a 56–5 victory. It was as good an exhibition of wet-weather rugby as I had witnessed. Midweek defeats of Moseley and Coventry, both by big margins, were followed by a 70–7 crushing of Gloucester at Kingsholm.

It would have made more sense for West Hartlepool to have played Romania and England to have faced Canterbury. Perhaps more to the point, the obvious opposition for provincial and state teams from the southern hemisphere are the English divisional sides. The current lamentable state of Romanian rugby can be gauged by the fact that in February their A team were beaten 97–14 by England Emerging Players at Brierton Lane. Far better, surely, for England's youngsters, effectively the national third string, to have been matched against the Ranfurly Shield holders.

But for once, it is not the constituent bodies we should blame entirely for the Canterbury debacle, though it is true that no time could apparently be found in an overcrowded season for any of the English divisions to meet the New Zealanders. Instead the CIS Divisional Championship proceeded without any of the England squad. They were excused on the grounds that since their international commitments would be extended into June, they should be allowed a mid-season break.

No one could reasonably quarrel with the decision to give the England men a couple of free weekends when the demands on their time were being taken to the limit. Yet by downgrading the regional tournament, the RFU provided more ammunition for those who argue that the administrators have created a hopeless muddle of representative rugby. There is a lack of focus and clarity. Not only is there too much rugby, but far too much of the representative element lacks essential purpose.

For almost a century the rock on which the game in England was founded was the County Championship, to which the clubs gave their unyielding support. The title was fought for with a relentless vigour rarely evident in friendly club fixtures. A good performance in the Championship was a player's passport to an England trial. Indeed, the England Grand Slam team of 1980 was solidly based on Bill Beaumont's Lancashire side, who lifted the County Championship that season. There were seven Lancastrians under the Fylde man's inspirational leadership who helped secure the first England Slam since 1957. Three of them – Fran Cotton, Steve Smith and Tony Neary – also captained England. What riches in a county team.

Mention those golden days and county officials go misty-eyed. Most appear oblivious to the revolution that is now taking place in the game. Times may be changing for some, but not for the counties. They want time to stand still. Their championship should be eternal. It doesn't take someone with Themistoclean foresight to realise that even in the world of nostalgia-perfumed rugby nothing is forever. The constituent bodies' most sacred cow ought to be led quietly to the abattoir and a peaceful death. Inevitably there will be some protesters willing to lie down in the road to prevent the slaughter; so be it.

The reforms ought not to stop there. It is almost 15 years since the playing sub-committee of the RFU produced their radical report on the need to restructure the game in England, at both club and representative level. The Burgess report, as it became known, recommended national club leagues and a divisional championship. It took England six more years to adopt the former, though this was partly due to the obstinacy of the counties, and the four-region competition has never been an unqualified success. Burgess was the precursor of a root-and-branch remodelling of the game in England. What we need now is not a similar royal commission on the state of English rugby: the changes taking place as the adult game embraces professionalism are driven by factors beyond the limited orbit of the authority retained by the constituent bodies. The major clubs, with their self-governing association, have already opted for Europe; the counties no longer have a direct say in the appointment of referees to National League matches. Discipline is still within their remit, but it is only a matter of time before the clubs in the top four Leagues demand control of this facet, once the concept of red and yellow cards leads to a totting-up arrangement.

It is elsewhere that the constituent bodies can still be a force for good. Some advances have been made with under-21 rugby. Most National League clubs run an under-21 team and there is an Under-21 County Championship, which should be vital in uncovering new talent. Regrettably, this competition contributes quite unnecessarily to the glut of demands being made on established players.

Yorkshire, who won the county under-21 title by beating Buckinghamshire 20–6, were able to call on ten players who had

The County Under-21 final, in which Yorkshire ran out 20–6 winners over Buckinghamshire.

James Naylor made regular first-team appearances for Orrell, yet still appeared for Yorkshire in the Under-21 County Championship.

represented England at various junior levels and a dozen who had played National League rugby for their clubs. James Naylor, first choice on Orrell's right wing, was among them. Quite clearly Naylor should not be required to play at this level when he has already acquired the skills which equip him for top-class club rugby. The petty empire-builders may not like it, but players who play National League rugby should be disbarred from under-21 county football, and from any of the student tournaments now crowding the congested calendar.

If the clutter of junior representative rugby merely invites disapproval, then the Under-21 Divisional Championship shames those responsible for its management. As Rob Andrew makes clear in his book *A Game and a Half*, watching under-21 inter-provincial matches in South Africa brings it home to us just how far away England are from treating under-21 rugby with the seriousness it deserves. In Australia, New Zealand and South Africa, centres of excellence have been established to develop the talent that is their countries' future. Here we play our Under-21 Divisional Championship on the Sundays following Five Nations matches. In the southern hemisphere, they play their under-21 games as curtain-raisers to major matches in their best stadia.

Inter-state rugby for these youngsters attracts the top coaches and is televised. Consequently, it enjoys a notably higher profile than its counterpart in England. It is also much better preparation for those with the capacity and aptitude for open-age international rugby. Is it any wonder, then, that talent in this country develops more slowly and is recognised so much later?

As long as the constituent bodies persist with the notion that there is still some merit in the County Championship, under-21 rugby – even at divisional level – will languish in a backwater. If the counties won't change of their own accord, then England's senior team management should take over the responsibility for running the Under-21 Divisional Championship themselves, just as they do the England A and Emerging Players squads.

For longer than is reasonable or can be justified, the constituent bodies have hindered rather than helped what progress there has been in representative rugby at all but the most junior levels. But if England are to have any chance of catching up with the southern hemisphere countries, they should divest themselves of the belief that the counties will willingly assist them.

THE RUGBY WORLD
CUP 1995

Wales in the World Cup and Beyond

by David Parry-Jones

At the death, there was just a single point in it – 23–24. That tiny margin, however, spelled exit for Wales from the 1995 World Cup at the hands of an exuberant Irish side who took second place in Pool C and went on from Ellis Park, Johannesburg to a quarter-final against France. Once again Wales, and Welsh rugby, were in crisis. Heavy gloom and despondency, which had seemed briefly to lift during the immediate build-up to the tournament, settled once more over the Land of the Dragon.

Defeat by Western Samoa in the pool stage of the 1991 competition had meant that the Welsh would not be seeded four years later. However, the new management team of Robert Norster and Alan Davies appeared for a time to have laid the foundations for some sorely needed stability. This regime reached its apogee with an admittedly fortuitous Five Nations title in 1994. Their side then went through a laborious World Cup qualifying period with wins over Portugal, Spain, Romania and Italy which placed them in Pool C in May 1995. Japan, New Zealand and Ireland would be

Wales had to suffer the ignominy of qualifying for the World Cup. Only their status as hosts has prevented them from having to tread a similar path in 1999.

Alex Evans was appointed Wales coach before the World Cup. Was he given enough time to have any influence on the course of events in South Africa?

their opponents, and there was the prospect of second place and progress to the knock-out stages.

Alas, there followed five successive Test defeats and a wooden spoon for the defending Five Nations champions, which led to the resignation of Norster and Davies. Alex Evans, a former assistant coach to successful Wallaby XVs and then under contract to the revitalised Cardiff RFC, accepted an offer to coach Wales through the World Cup. The manager would be Geoff Evans, a 1971 British Lion, with Mike Ruddock of Swansea and Dennis John of Pontypridd on board to complete what was undoubtedly a powerful controlling group.

These men had only weeks in which to re-inject *hwyl* and give direction to demoralised players. The squad which they soon named contained surprises, such as the uncapped Cardiffian Andy Moore at scrum-half plus untried youngsters in Bridgend's Gareth Thomas and student full-back Justin Thomas. But there were also men of huge experience in Robert Jones, Gareth Llewellyn and Ieuan Evans, though the captaincy was stripped from the latter and given to the Cardiff skipper, Mike Hall.

The early vibes were encouraging. Before his party flew to South Africa on 16 May, Alex Evans felt able to state that they lacked nothing in skill and physique compared with England and the southern hemisphere giants. His manager added that Wales were destined to go far in the tournament.

Their hotel in the small but attractive city of Bloemfontein was idyllic, built as a two-storey quadrangle around lawns and a pool. Here the players lazed in the warm sunshine after energetic training sessions which often alarmed onlookers by their sheer violence. Evans controlled them with short, sharp whistles, fingers between teeth, for all the world like a Welsh mountain shepherd working his dogs. The players began to smile again; they were relaxed; the confidence that they had re-acquired was evident. After a week, acclimatisation to the 4,000ft altitude was complete.

Japan were seen off comfortably enough. Before a crowd of 25,000 at the Free State Stadium, Wales ran up 54 points, debutant Gareth Thomas registering a hat-trick, Ieuan Evans crossing twice, Moore and Taylor adding further tries, and Neil Jenkins contributing the balance with his reliable boot. Despite conceding two tries to the hard-running wing Oto, the Dragons seemed to have got their act together. They flew buoyantly into Johannesburg, where they were based at another excellent hotel to prepare for the midweek evening tie against New Zealand.

Injuries forced Alex Evans to recast his preferred back line, with Neil Jenkins reverting to fly-half from the No. 12 berth he had filled against Japan and Proctor posted on the wing outside Thomas. Robert Jones came in at scrum-half behind a pack in which Greg Prosser was awarded a first cap at lock and Gareth Llewellyn moved to the flank. The selection of Jonathan Humphreys at hooker completed a bid to field maximum height and brawn against the All Blacks at Ellis Park.

Under brilliant floodlights Wales led briefly through a dropped goal by Jenkins (who later kicked two penalties). But in the second quarter New Zealand took complete control. Little and Ellis scored tries, Andrew Mehrtens adding ten points with the boot. The Welsh pack strove manfully in the second half, John Davies and Derwyn Jones shining, but a Josh Kronfeld try after bulky New Zealand newcomer Lomu had brushed Proctor out of his way, plus nine more points from Mehrtens, completed the execution.

There was, however, still a bullish outlook as Wales took the field three days later, but when Ireland began in traditional banshee fashion the Dragons played like men bewitched. Elwood's conversions of soft tries by Popplewell and McBride established a 14–0 lead after 15 minutes and from then it was catch-up rugby for Hall and his men. Adrian Davies dropped a goal and Jenkins kicked two penalties and converted tries by Humphreys and Taylor, but it was too little, too late. A try by Halvey and more accurate place-kicking by Elwood kept Ireland just of reach until the close.

Afterwards, in the changing room, Welsh faces were white, drawn and expressionless. They knew they had underperformed. They had blown it.

Wales enjoyed their only victory in South Africa against Japan. All in all, it was a dismal World Cup for the Dragons.

Ironically, they would not have to qualify for 1999, since the WRU would be hosting the tournament. Small consolation.

As supporters' tongues began wagging at the start of what promised to be a four-year talking shop, there were only questions, not answers. Why had a gifted, well-drilled squad failed to deliver even a face-saving quarter-final place? Should Alex Evans be asked to continue as coach after endorsing the lengthy 22 drop-outs that afforded free balls to the Irish counter-attackers? If invited, would he take the job? Should the search be intensified for the elusive 'Welsh style', transferring the thrust point to the area around outside centre and away from the ruck-and-maul situations where today's giant-sized opponents thrive? Is there too much negative coaching at club level? Should domestic League rugby, conditioning teams to the avoidance of defeat and relegation, be put under the microscope? How, in short, can the standing of a once-great rugby nation be restored?

Since rugby is a players' game, the principal answers surely lie with the present, and next, generation. The players relish fame, glamour, generous expenses and perks, but these, gentlemen, have to be earned – by blood, sweat, tears and results. To pull on the red jersey of Wales goes some way to conferring heroic status on a mere mortal. But it can only be the start of a journey to glory.

THEMBA'S T-SHIRT
AND OTHER TALES

BY JOHN INVERDALE

His name was Themba, he came from Jo'burg, as Barry Manilow might have said, and he had no interest in rugby. I knew that because the first time we met, as he carried my bags up to my hotel room, he shot me a rather quizzical glance. 'You here for the rugby? I got no interest in rugby.'

Five weeks later, he came up to my room to take those same bags down to Reception just one last time. It was World Cup final day. I had one remaining clean T-shirt, which marked South Africa's opening victory over Australia – Springboks pictured doing things to Wallabies that probably aren't allowed. 'Please,' he begged, 'can I have that T-shirt? Today is the proudest day of my life. My country are playing in the World Cup final. I want to wear something that shows how proud I am.'

All of which made me rather proud too – proud and privileged to have been part of such a fantastic, truly historic sporting event which brought people together and showed the world Rugby Union at its best. And it also explains why I was forced to appear in a crumpled only-worn-four-times-in-the-past-week shirt at Ellis Park on that great day.

For BBC Radio, it was a strange sort of tournament because we were very conscious that some people were listening to us with the television sound turned down, just to hear Bill McLaren. On a news

'Catch me if you can.' Few players could pin down Jonah Lomu during the course of the World Cup.

and sport network this did sometimes create the odd problem, because, short of Bill chairing Prime Minister's Question Time, there was the occasional conflict of interest, and when John Major decided that the second half of the England–France game was just so dreadful he had to resign, ITV's John Taylor, not John Redwood, was one of the chief beneficiaries.

A sky-diver enters the Ellis Park Stadium during the closing ceremony.

Running alongside such hitches was the interminable hunger, 24 hours a day, for material. From the first day, we were getting endless requests for 'a chat with Jack Rowell at six o'clock in the morning', 'those four Ivory Coast supporters who paint their faces', 'someone to explain that Western Samoan war dance', 'someone to explain the line-out laws'. Not a soul could be found who could provide an adequate answer to that last one.

And then... and then... there was Jonah Lomu. After the Ireland game,

Radio 4 wanted to speak to him. 'What do you mean, he's not doing interviews?' Which meant that we spoke to everyone and anyone who had ever so much as got within touching distance of Jonah – hence not too many of his opposite numbers – and Radio New Zealand's Graham Moody became an authority on his schooldays, his parents, his church, his pets, his car, his friends. When Jonah claims his millions, he owes Graham a few Kiwi dollars. On the other hand, the England and Scotland squads were a broadcaster's dream, available morning, noon and night, on the most spurious of pretexts, to talk about almost anything. Even rugby. After the Scotland against Tonga match, Charles Runcie, a cross between Fleagle in *Banana Splits* and Rab C. Nesbitt, was dispatched into the Scotland dressing room for the usual 'how I scored a try' interview.

Every player was naked – and Charles had to take one of them to the interview/camera position where their chat would be beamed to all the press and all the televisions in the ground. Persuading someone to put back on a rather mangled and slightly unhygienic jockstrap for the purposes of a three-minute radio interview is not something they teach you on training courses. Eric Peters eventually relented, and Charles, who rather touchingly wore the same Radio 5 rugby shirt every day of the tournament, could claim another notable coup.

There is one huge psychological problem that has to be overcome on major sporting occasions, though: how to keep fit yourself. It's rather disconcerting to be in a bar surrounded by Welsh or Irish internationals, supreme examples of the human form, on the eve of a Test, and to see them sipping orange juice, while you, arm twisted firmly behind your back, are halfway through a fourth pint of Guinness. So I went running in downtown Johannesburg. And once I'd done it once, it was easy. Most days, in the no-go Hillbrow area where our hotel was conveniently situated, I set off. Was there ever a bigger incentive to run fast? I think not. 'You got something wrong with your head doing that round here,' said one old lady at a set of traffic lights. And schoolchildren laughed in a pitying sort of way. Undeterred, I carried on, getting geared up for 'our' big match, which would feature the journalists and broadcasters of the northern hemisphere against their counterparts from the south.

When your playing career has taken the word ignominious to previously unplumbed depths, moments like the one I enjoyed before that game will linger long in the memory. We played at the Rand University ground, capacity 14,000, crowd 13,900 less than that. We met in the dressing room. Two of us had a slight tiff over the No. 15 jersey. Me and Serge Blanco.

'Serge,' j'ai dis. 'Moi quinze, vous dix, OK?'

'OK,' he said.

He made an old man very happy. 'Did I ever tell you about the time I got selected in South Africa – on the eve of the World Cup final, may I say – at full-back ahead of Serge Blanco... ?' But the day afterwards was even more memorable, were that possible. The media as a whole are regarded as a rather gnarled and cynical old bunch without a good word to say about anything or anyone. To see some of that chosen number dabbing tears from their eyes at the final whistle was a sight I'll long remember. And to see 500 women from the townships forming an impromptu choir in the departure area of Jan Smuts International Airport to sing their new anthem and to celebrate their real arrival on the international sporting stage was a moment to treasure.

I bought a T-shirt at the airport to see me home. It's stuffed in a drawer somewhere now. I hope – all these months on – that Themba's still got his.

Helicopters fly past Ellis Park before the final.

A Magnificent Rugby Occasion

by Clem Thomas

The third World Cup, held in South Africa, was another tremendous success and further propelled Rugby Union football to its unstated objective of becoming a major world game. For that is surely what World Cups are all about. Nevertheless, one came away with the impression that the tournament was more memorable for the occasion and the event itself, rather than for the quality of the rugby which, for the most part, was modest. That is not to say that we did not see some deeply absorbing, highly competitive and exciting games and some fine individual performances.

Nelson Mandela at the World Cup final wearing a replica No. 6 shirt given to him by François Pienaar. South Africa's success symbolised the coming together of a once-divided nation.

The result was the best possible one for the host nation, who seemed to stage-manage the whole affair to perfection. There were some dark whispers suggesting they had done exactly that. I prefer the theory that South Africa were carried along on a floodtide of national spirit and emotion which could not be denied, and which helped bond the concept of a country given a fresh start, based on the marvellous philosophies of that magical man, Nelson Mandela, and his followers, who so generously offered a spirit of reconciliation to people who had made one of the gravest errors in the history of mankind by introducing the wicked policy of apartheid.

If all South Africa's objectives were virtually met by winning that dream final against New Zealand, their greatest rivals for world supremacy, which threw their rugby-mad nation into ecstasy, other nations' ambitions bit the dust so resoundingly that the disappointment will take a long time to get over. Australia, the holders and worthy champions for four years, fell at the first hurdle, the match following the amazing opening ceremony in Cape Town. Those of us who were there will never forget that occasion because of the deep emotions it generated and the dignity imposed upon it by the presence of Nelson Mandela, arguably the greatest African leader of all time. Although they lost by the narrowest of margins, one sensed that Australia were not the side they had been and that many of their players had gone a bridge too far; instinctively, one knew that they were not going to win.

Similarly England, whose best moment was putting paid to Australia in the quarter-final, to the utter disgust of the Wallabies' sledger-in-chief, David Campese, were far from convincing and looked sluggish on the firm going. As expected by most of their critics, their slow and giraffe-like back row was finally annihilated in the semi-final by All Black warthogs such as Kronfeld, who cleaned them out for ground ball. The ground conditions were critical. As the sun shone on the hard pitches of the high veld and, strangely, on the more temperate fields of Western Province, the southern hemisphere countries flourished because of the speed of their game, while the British teams, reared on the heavy grounds and rainy weather of the British winter, quickly found themselves so far off the pace that the argument of whether we in the British Isles should play our rugby at a different time of the year was reopened.

Perversely, the only exception to the fine weather was Durban, where they say it never rains in May or June and where England played their pool games. Some gremlin or other decided to invoke Sod's Law and it rained for most of the time. The weather had an influential effect on that crucial semi-final between France and South Africa, a match which, in my opinion, should never have been played. The World Cup officials seemed determined that it should go ahead for the sake of expediency, and dare I say they all wanted to be in Cape Town the next day for the other semi-final between New Zealand and England. In the event, the final arbiter, the referee, Derek Bevan, was persuaded to allow the game to continue after a two-hour delay, during which we saw the remarkable spectacle of an army of black Mrs Mops attempting to sweep away the oceans of standing water. Where on earth did they all come from?

The semi-final gave the French more reason to be aggrieved than any team in the

Aubin Hueber gets the ball away for France during their quarter-final clash with Ireland. In the subsequent semi-final in Durban, the French flair was clearly restricted by the downpour.

tournament because, as you can imagine, the conditions scarcely favoured them. They like to play at risk in the open field, and love to counter-attack with that extravagant flamboyancy and flair which has won them countless games – including the recent Second Test in New Zealand, when they scored one of the great tries of all time to win the two-match series. To add to their woes, almost every decision went against them and, when they forced three successive scrums on the Springbok line in the closing minutes and signalled their intention of going for a pushover from the second by throwing 11 men into the push, the scrum was collapsed. Bevan deemed that it was not a penalty try and the great relief of the home fans was tangible as the Springboks scraped through to their dream final.

Conversely, the other semi-final, at Newlands between England and New Zealand, was played in perfect conditions and was far more one-sided. The initial assault by the All Blacks saw them put 25 points on the board in fewer minutes. England were crushed by the pace and by New Zealand's new secret weapon, Jonah Lomu.

The pool games virtually confirmed the seedings, the only real upset coming in that memorable opening game at Newlands, when the Springboks sensationally gave notice of their enormous determination with that 27–18 victory over the holders. If Australia were out of sorts, then the same thing could be said of England in Pool B, which was a nasty part of the draw, for it contained the warriors Western Samoa and the two best unseeded teams in the competition, Italy and Argentina. However, they struggled through and, although they played their best rugby to beat Australia in the quarter-final, again one sensed that they were not in the hunt.

Pool C contained the Samurai-brave but too diminutive Japanese and two of the Four Home Union sides, Ireland and Wales, who were the most ineffective of all and could be ranked among the poorer teams of the tournament. In fact, the Wales–Ireland game, which decided who would go through to the quarters, was voted as easily the worst game of the whole competition. Some mitigation could be offered for Wales, as it was generally accepted that they were represented by their second team, due to the depredations of the professional League. Cruising among them was the killer shark New Zealand, who gobbled them up with no trouble at all and then, on the flimsy evidence of having beaten all Four Home Union teams, became the firm favourites to win the Cup. It appeared that South Africa in the final were the first serious competition they would meet.

In the fourth pool the dominant team was France, with Scotland putting up a respectable show. You could see that France were gaining

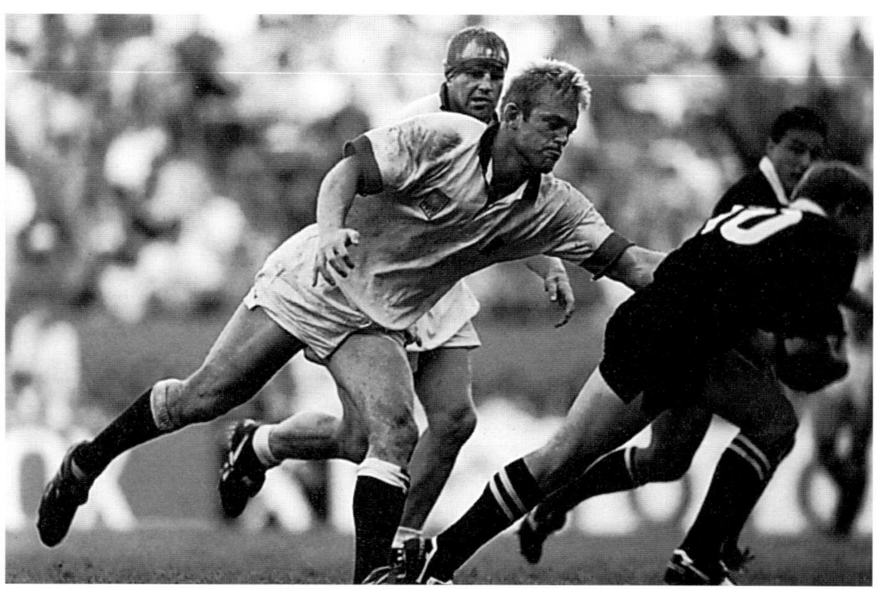

All Black Andrew Mehrtens evades the grasp of Tim Rodber. England could not cope with the pace and power of the Kiwis.

strength as they progressed; as Pierre Berbizier, their coach, said, 'We are capable of playing champagne rugby, but we have not yet got the cork out of the bottle.' The Ivory Coast were not serious opposition, and called into doubt a seeding procedure that allowed countries like the United States and Fiji to be excluded.

The quarters also went according to expectations, and although South Africa had a hard struggle against Western Samoa, France and New Zealand easily disposed of Ireland and Scotland.

The final saw a great victory by the Springboks, achieved not because they were the better side but through sheer persistence and a tremendous determination to win. They were willed on by the spirit of the whole nation, both white and black, and, above all, by the presence and support of Nelson Mandela, who at Ellis Park wore the No. 6 jersey of François Pienaar, South Africa's captain, as he was presented to the teams. It was a game lost by New Zealand rather than won by South Africa, and Andrew Mehrtens will be haunted for evermore by that missed drop-kick in the last minute of ordinary time, which drifted wide and took the game into extra time. It allowed the super-fit Springboks to dredge up one last effort of spirit to win the match and send the whole nation into paroxysms of delight. It was truly a magnificent rugby occasion which left many indelible memories in the minds of all who were there.

Some of the more outstanding memories of the tournament include the marvellous weather for rugby football and the fact that South Africa boasts so many superb rugby stadia. The sheer majesty of grounds such as Ellis Park, Loftus Versfeld, King's Park, Newlands, Crusaders and the New Free State Stadium at Bloemfontein has to be seen to be believed, as does the great beauty of smaller venues like Stellenbosch, so beloved by Danie Craven, which staged its first international, between Australia and Romania.

The worst moment was the terrible injury to Max Brito of Ivory Coast who was paralysed as a result of a freak accident in the match against Tonga. Another sour occasion was the brawl in the game between Canada and South Africa, which became known as the Battle of Boet Erasmus.

The worst games were Wales versus Ireland, England against France in the play-off for third place, in which neither team were much interested after the disappointment of losing their semis, and the Tonga–Ivory Coast game, for its horrific injury toll.

The outstanding personality of the tournament was, without question, the remarkable Jonah Lomu, whose Frankenstein physique, allied to great pace and rugby acumen, had some of the best coaches in the world reaching for the smelling salts and the valium as they racked their brains for a method of stopping him. After he had destroyed England, Will Carling said, 'I hope to never see him again!' More ironically, Tony Underwood,

South Africa parade the William Webb Ellis Trophy before an ecstatic Ellis Park crowd.

before having to mark him, declared, 'I'm not losing any sleep over Lomu.' Colin Meads, the All Black manager, said that he had seen players as big, but never on the wing. The best quote came from Lomu himself. When they asked who could stop him, he replied, 'Mum.' We are going to hear a great deal more of this extraordinary young man, who has been called a rugby freak.

There were other fine individual performances by the All Blacks, not least being the great centre play of Walter Little and the style of the quality young backs such as fly-half Andrew Mehrtens, Jeff Wilson and Glen Osborne. Their most impressive forwards were Zinzan Brooke, Josh Kronfeld and Olo Brown. South Africa had no lesser heroes in their electrifying scrum-half Joost van der Westhuizen, their magnificently composed and suave full-back, André Joubert, and Mark Andrews and Du Randt in the pack. France contributed fine players in Ntamack, Lacroix, Cabannes and Benazzi. The best Australian was their magnificent lock, John Eales.

The greatest rugby of the tournament came from the All Blacks, but only against indifferent opposition, and once they played some big boys, they came adrift. Another marvellous memory is the splendid back play of the Western Samoans, which, strangely, flourished even behind a woeful pack of forwards. Some of the best forward play came from Argentina, who taught both England and Samoa a thing or two. The funniest story concerned England, Wales and Argentina, who shared a plane for the trip to the inaugural lunch in Cape Town. On the way home, the aircraft struck an air pocket and dropped a few hundred feet, scaring the passengers out of their wits. Apparently one of the first to recover was the Welsh coach, Australian Alex Evans, who exclaimed, 'I don't mind going down with these English bastards, but I'm a bit afraid that the Argies will eat me!'

In the background the spectre of professionalism lurked, and when, midway through the tournament, it was announced that the three southern hemisphere countries had agreed a deal with Rupert Murdoch giving them some $700 million over ten years, it was virtually official that Rugby Union, after 172 years, had become professional, even though the International Board were not meeting until the end of August to consider the matter. Once again the southern hemisphere countries had pre-empted the situation, just as they had done when they forced the northern hemisphere to accept the concept of a World Cup.

The only thing left to work out now is how to give the players what they deserve, and at the same time keep enough money to propagate the game. It is imperative that neither side becomes greedy.

Burto's Bashers XV –
Europe's Most Successful
World Cup Team?

BY MIKE BURTON

The beauty of a British Lions tour is that all the people are travelling to the same place at the same time to support the same team. Yes, English, Welsh, Scots or Irish, they all want the Lions to win. A World Cup tour, on the other hand, presents a host of problems and situations which cannot be legislated for in advance. For example, if England had lost to Western Samoa in Durban, their quarter-final would have been in Johannesburg, which would have been slightly inconvenient for all those who had made travel arrangements to Cape Town and booked hotel accommodation in the same fair city. Although many of the pool matches were wholly predictable, who could have forecast that Scotland would go down by that last-minute try to France, and who could have hazarded a guess between Ireland and Wales to take on France in the Durban quarter-final? If England hadn't gone to Cape Town, how would the thousands of people travelling in my party have seen Table Mountain, Stellenbosch and the Wine Trail?

Months before departure I had checked the booking lists, and with nowhere to hedge my bets, I gambled on England scraping home against Western Samoa, France doing the same against Scotland and, because more Welsh people than Irish had booked on our tour to Durban, I was confident that Wales would murder Ireland 3–0.

Experience tells me that the hotels can be perfect, all the flights on time, the coach transfers immaculate, but if the party cannot see their heroes play, then riot is imminent.

Large groups of Welsh supporters arrived in Durban via Johannesburg in time to meet their team boarding the plane home. But no problem, Burto had the answer. For years now, on all the rugby and cricket tours I organise, Burto's Bashers, a scratch team made up of people on the tour with me, have taken on the locals. We had not won a cricket match in either the West Indies or Australia, and the last time we looked like getting a result at rugby was against Canterbury Contemptibles in Christchurch during the 1993 Lions tour, when an over-zealous referee from Otago slayed us with a last-minute penalty against our openside for cowardice in the face of the

Anguish or pain? Steve Ojomoh leaves the field suffering from a facial injury during England's Pool B encounter with Argentina in the World Cup.

Surf's up! Rory
Underwood, Phil
de Glanville,
Tony Underwood
and Kyran
Bracken find time
to relax in
Durban.

Will Carling and his England team stand up to the All Blacks' *haka*. Unfortunately for England, the World Cup semi-final was out of their reach after a blistering opening ten minutes.

Ireland's Denis McBride is hauled out of the ruck by Welsh flanker Stuart Davies in the last Pool C encounter in South Africa. The match was one of the poorest games of the tournament.

THE HEART OF ASIA

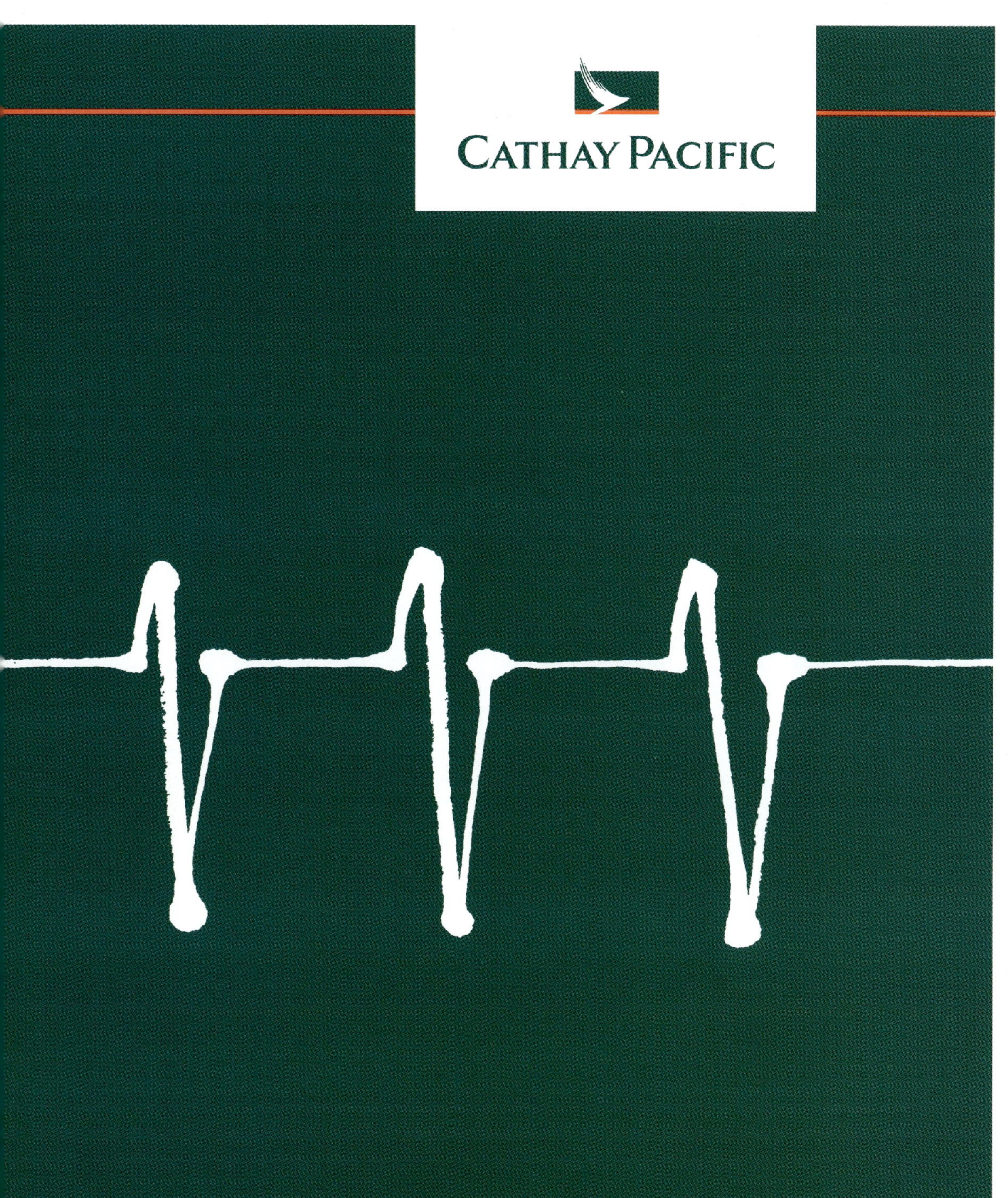

CATHAY PACIFIC
...eek to and from Hong Kong. Cathay Pacific. The Heart of Asia.

Scottish
supporters show
the South African
crowd the secrets
of Highland
dancing before the
Pool D encounter
with Tonga.

The magnificent Hong Kong Stadium. With a capacity of 40,000, it is truly a worthy venue for the Rugby World Cup Sevens in 1997.

A welcome from the rainbow nation. Dancers entertain the crowd at the opening ceremony of the Rugby World Cup.

LOCAL STRENGTH. FULLY INTERNATIONAL.

The top players have a number of things in common.

Experience of playing conditions around the world. A capacity to read the game. A sense of teamwork. Strength. Speed. And, above all, the ability to make fast decisions.

HongkongBank

The Hongkong and Shanghai Banking Corporation Limited

Fast decisions. Worldwide.

enemy. The simple midfield kick saw us to a 27–28 defeat.

Knowing that Scots, English, Welsh and Irish supporters arriving for the quarter-finals of the World Cup might see their team play only once, I set about arranging a six-match programme for Burto's Bashers XV, three games in Durban and three games in Cape Town. In a move designed to terrify the opposition, the players were kitted out in full Springbok green and gold. This had no effect on a Collegians third XV who beat us in the first match under floodlights on a superb ground adjacent to King's Park. The second game brought victory and the third match, at Glenwood Old Boys against an invitation coloured XV, was magnificent. Again, it was played under floodlights and an encounter with plenty of movement and pace resulted in a win for Burto's Bashers. To think that this was just a rags team. What would happen if they were properly coached?

So we arrived in Cape Town for the last three matches, against a Cape Select XV (easy, 34 points), a Hamilton's President's XV (not so easy but still a win), and the notorious Buccaneers. The last side were due to face us in the final game of the tour the day before England played New Zealand in their ill-fated semi-final. Because of the four-wins-to-one ratio, Burto's

Burto's Bashers XV line up before their match against the Collegians third XV. The Springbok kit was designed to intimidate the opposition.

Bashers had become a feared outfit, prowling the Cape in Springbok gear. John Hulse, the Buccanneers' supremo, had got wind of our prowess and had beefed up his 'fun side' to produce a mean and pacy bunch determined to uphold the honour of Cape Province.

I had forgotten to tell him that Mike Teague was arriving with one of our groups for the later stages of the tour, and we quietly slipped him in at No. 8. In addition, the large form of Richard Bath, the editor of *Rugby News*, had led several other groups of supporters into Cape Town for the semis. His presence in the middle of the line-out ensured possession which M. Teague turned into points with a 40-yard dash to score under the posts. And so, with the final a week away, England and France were the only European teams in with a chance of being as successful in South Africa in 1995 as Burto's Bashers. History will record that France won the play-off at Loftus Versfeld, which meant that of the six games they played they lost one, to South Africa, thereby equalling Burto's Bashers' record of won 5, lost 1.

England had played six, but having gone down to France and New Zealand, would have finished below Burto's Bashers had the 1995 World Cup been decided on a league basis. Upon my return to England's green and pleasant land, reflecting upon South Africa '95 I think of the epic train journey we took from Cape Town to Johannesburg; of Table Mountain; of the great sights and sounds of the South African game parks; of the long beaches of Durban; of the hospitality of every South African citizen we met. These memories are punctuated by a nagging doubt as to where that Collegians' third team would have finished in the 1995 World Cup.

The Springbok kit had little effect on the outcome of the game, but great fun was had by all.

ON THE HOME FRONT

GAVIN HASTINGS – LEADING FROM THE FRONT

BY BILL McLAREN

It would be hard to find anyone who has typified Scottish sporting prowess more than Andrew Gavin Hastings, who has retired from international Rugby Union after a glittering career that began with a match-winning haul of six penalty goals in the 18–17 Murrayfield defeat of France in 1986 and ended with another six goals against the mighty All Blacks in the quarter-final of the 1995 World Cup in South Africa.

No one has been better equipped for the modern game in the 1980s and 1990s, nor has adorned the game with such grace, power, competitiveness and integrity. He has the ideal build for a modern full-back, at 6ft 2in and just under 15st, and is handsome enough to make girls' hearts flutter; his love of his country, athleticism, skill and resolve have so suited him to the role of world-class rugby player that he became a household name wherever the game is played, a man revered and respected all over the world. New Zealanders call a spade a spade and do not award accolades lightly. You have to earn their respect and admiration. It was testimony to the personality and character of Gavin Hastings that, as captain of the British Lions in New Zealand in 1993, he was accorded the highest praise as hard-bitten Kiwis took him to their hearts – yes, even the newspaper columnists who usually give visiting rugby men a hard time.

Of course, it stood to reason that A.G. Hastings would be a highly motivated sportsman. After all, as one of four brothers whose father, Clifford, was an outstanding Watsonians and Edinburgh forward stalwart, he had to hold his own in the rough and tumble of combat in a very sports-orientated family. That competitive urge never has left him, and he has set alongside his desire to win a personal target of always reaching for his own highest potential.

One of his most impressive qualities is courage. In the modern game more than ever before, full-backs have to

The pinnacle of an illustrious career. Gavin Hastings leads out the British Lions for the First Test against the All Blacks at Lancaster Park, Christchurch.

be brave. Time and again you see a forlorn figure gazing upwards at the mortar bomb descending upon him as the sound of enemy hoofbeats grows ever louder. Gavin Hastings never flinched. His judgement of whether to remain on the ground or to leap up to make the catch and perhaps to get dumped from on high never wavered. He was in every respect a players' player who was at the very heart of Scottish endeavour in a remarkable resurgence from despair to delight, from failure to heartening success. At the start of the 1994–5 season Scotland had played nine games without a win. There was sadness in the land. Since then they have won eight internationals and lost only to the heavyweights, England, France and New Zealand. Gavin Hastings was the key figure in that uplifting transformation. His scoring feats are already embedded in Rugby Union lore. He held the world record of 44 points in an international until the New Zealander Simon Culhane scored 45 against Japan in the World Cup. Hastings leads the overall World Cup scoring list with 227 points in three tournaments. He has scored more international points (667) than any other northern hemisphere player and lies second only to Australia's Michael Lynagh (894) in the all-time world list. He is Scotland's most-capped player, having gained his 61st against New Zealand in the 1995 World Cup. He has captained Scotland in 20 internationals and he and his brother Scott have set a world mark by appearing together in 51 Scottish Tests.

Gavin Hastings and Kenny Logan celebrate the Scotland captain's sensational last-minute try against France. It was Scotland's first win in Paris for 26 years.

Of his many feats of derring-do, perhaps that against France in the 1995 Five Nations Championship will live longest in the memory, for it was truly the stuff of legend. France had just taken the lead. No-side was approaching. Captain Hastings gathers his disciples around him and in quiet, matter-of-fact tones, he tells them: 'Now, come on boys, let's get up to the other end, score between the posts and I'll kick the goal.' Straight out of a Hollywood script, he thundered 40 metres for a glorious try (his record 17th as Scotland full-back) and kicked the conversion that gave Scotland victory by 23–21, their first win in Paris for 26 years. He simply radiated confidence as an inspiration to his colleagues.

Thoroughly approachable, he has that gift for conveying to folk that he is enjoying conversing with them. He has dealt with constant demands from the media with tolerance and patience. He hasn't

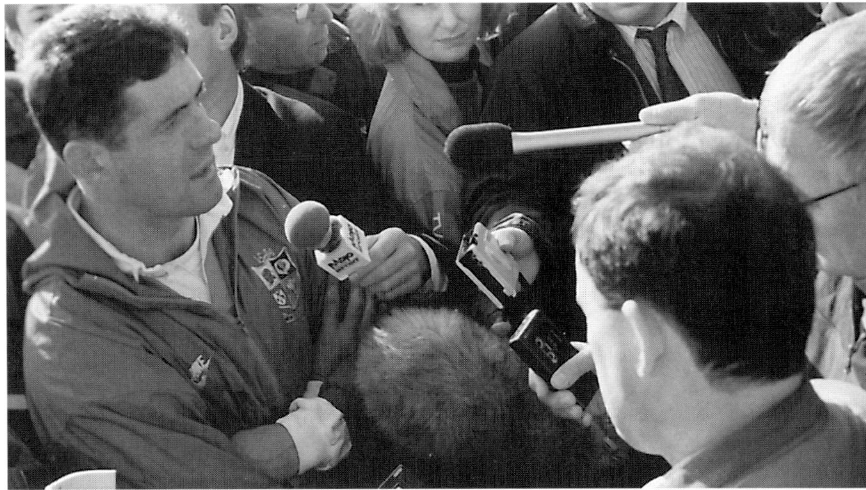

boasted, he hasn't belittled. He has approached every situation and judged it as he saw it with fairness and integrity, feet firmly planted. Asked about his record 44 points, he replied that, while he was glad to have made such a contribution, it was, after all, his job in what was in every sense a team effort. When subjected to criticism at a press conference after the 34–12 defeat by South Africa in November 1994, one journalist asking if he did not consider himself to be too old and too slow, Gavin said, 'Gosh, I'll lose a lot of sleep over that comment.' It spoke volumes for his determination and dedication that he emerged from that spell of back trouble and doubt to play some of the best rugby of his career. It seemed appropriate that he should take his leave of the international scene with a display at once spirited, committed and inspiring, for although Scotland lost to New Zealand in the World Cup quarter-final by 30–48, theirs was a heartening effort in which they equalled the record of David Sole's 1990 Scotland side in scoring three tries in an international against the All Blacks.

In making such a mighty impact upon the Scottish sporting scene, Gavin Hastings has proved the ideal role model for young Scots to seek to emulate. Listen to Jim Telfer, Scotland's coaching director and not one given to lavish praise: 'Gavin's contribution, on and off the field, has been immense. He is an excellent ambassador for Scotland. In personal habits and behaviour he sets a superb example. He looks after himself, is always fit; he leads from the front, players respond to him and his skills are as good as ever. At home and abroad he demonstrates always the very best side of the Scottish character.'

That really says it all.

ENGLAND'S DILEMMA

BY PAUL ACKFORD

So that's that. Four years down the pan. All those training sessions, fine words and detailed plans did not do the trick. Instead of mastering the world of rugby, England finished a dismal fourth. Although the management team of Jack Rowell, John Elliott and Les Cusworth were reluctant to admit it publicly, the unpalatable conclusion has to be that England are still a good few steps behind the world's best with little prospect of catching up.

Several senior players dismissed the semi-final performance against New Zealand as an exceptional – non-repeatable – aberration. Take that Jonah Lomu out of the game, they said, and it would have been different. And in any case, we won the second half 26–20, didn't we? That analysis is hopelessly and completely wrong. It is understandable coming from players who have to repair shattered dreams, but when Rowell also subscribes to the theory, as he did immediately after the match, then English rugby really is in trouble.

To make matters worse, Rowell continued to talk up England's World

England coach Jack Rowell. Should he shoulder some of the blame for England's showing in the World Cup?

Cup weeks after the tournament had ended. 'I don't go along with the view that England have had a disappointing World Cup,' he said. 'It was a big let-down losing in the semi-final, but I think the campaign should be viewed as a very respectable showing. On the basis that we came to the tournament to learn, we have seen a style of play and movement to which we aspire.' Rowell listed various reasons – excuses? – why the game in this country still has a long way to go before it can hold its head high. 'We need to be involved with New Zealand, Australia and South Africa on an annual basis,' he said. 'To play Australia for the first time after a gap of four years isn't good for Australia or England.'

Fair enough, if this were true, but it is not. Confronting southern hemisphere sides is exactly what England have been doing in recent seasons. The England A team has just returned from a trip to Australia, where they beat Australia A; the All Blacks were in England in 1993; most of the England players were with the Lions in New Zealand the same year; England travelled to South Africa last season and the Springboks are playing an international at the start of the 1995–6 season at Twickenham. So it is difficult to imagine a three-year stint in which senior England sides could have had more contact with the big three. And in any case, this southern hemisphere infatuation nonsense will not do. Before the World Cup semi-final the England players were saying that, having conquered Australia, New Zealand and South Africa recently, the southern hemisphere voodoo was a thing of the past. For far too long England have installed the southern hemisphere as the holy grail of international rugby without examining the reasons for doing so.

According to Rowell and Cusworth, the backs' coach, another problem is the poor playing conditions in England, which make it difficult to play this expansive game they have talked about for so long. 'We have just come through a Five Nations Championship in the third-wettest winter ever,' said Rowell. 'You come out to South Africa on these wonderful surfaces and it is a different matter altogether.' This analysis would have had a chance of standing up if England had played fluent rugby throughout the tournament. They did not, and the one side who did, New Zealand, endure equally filthy conditions during their own winter.

The fact remains that England were well prepared for this competition. Everything Rowell asked for, he was given. Most of the World Cup squad were rested, having missed several League games in April. They had something like 70 training sessions before the semi-final to get themselves ready, yet they played their worst 30 minutes of rugby for years in that match and followed it with an appalling first half against France. Even if

Big is beautiful – or is it? Tim Rodber is tackled by Robin Brooke in England's World Cup semi-final drubbing by the All Blacks. Rodber failed to display his Five Nations form during the tournament.

you accept that New Zealand are exceptional (not borne out by their display in the final) and that France have improved out of sight on their Five Nations form, England still underperformed by their own high standards. Rowell must shoulder a large chunk of the blame because for the first time in his rugby career he was unable to galvanise a team. For all their supposedly fine work on the training pitch, England disappointed badly during their matches.

So what's to be done? First, England have to deny their recent history. Big is no longer beautiful, and the practice of selecting monsters among the forwards and telling them to tilt at defences for 80 minutes is no longer valid. Tim Rodber and Victor Ubogu, so effective during the Five Nations, struggled in the World Cup; they were far too predictable and ultimately not powerful enough. England must also place a higher premium on skill.

Several of the Japanese players were technically far superior to their English counterparts. Forget about sports psychologists, nutritionists and technical advisers; get the players used to running with the ball rather than trying to kick the cover off it.

Rob Andrew has been a wonderful servant to England over the years but he was cruelly exposed in his last two matches. If England have genuine pretensions to challenging the best in the world, then they must start rebuilding their back line. And quickly. That advice is always greeted with the question, where is the next generation? It is exactly the question New Zealand asked of themselves before they threw Andrew Mehrtens, Glen Osborne and Lomu into the pot. There was some debate in New Zealand over whether any of them should have made the trip, and look how they turned out.

In England we are so concerned with identifying and developing players in the various England nursery teams that by the time they break into the national side they are either 104 years old or have had all their bravado and daring coached out of them. Rowell carries the can because of his position, but English rugby shares the responsibility, and unless there is a major shift in attitude and approach from players up and down the country, England will continue merely to pick up the odd Grand Slam, which means nothing when it comes to winning World Cups.

Andrew Mehrtens, the exciting fly-half, emerged as one of the new generation of All Blacks. Should England be following the example set by New Zealand?

RUGBY WORLDWIDE

THE TOURS

BY BILL MITCHELL

With the World Cup less than a year away there was much feverish activity on the international scene as countries sent out their hopefuls with a view to gaining much-needed experience. In September and October 1994 Argentina were in South Africa, where they had mixed results, being soundly beaten in two Tests and winning only three of their six matches. There was, however, one bizarre twist, which came in the Second Test when fly-half José Cilley was flown in to fill a vacancy, arrived a matter of hours before the kick-off and scored 21 of his side's points on his international debut.

The United States – by then out of the World Cup – took Namibia's place for a tour of Ireland in November 1994 and lost three matches out of four. Yet in the international they exposed weaknesses in the host country, which surprised no one. At the same time Romania paid a short visit to England and their performances in preliminaries against Oxford University (lost 16–26) and Cambridge University (won 27–18) scarcely impressed critics. Against England at Twickenham, they duly lost 54–3.

The United States in possession against Ireland during their short trip in November.

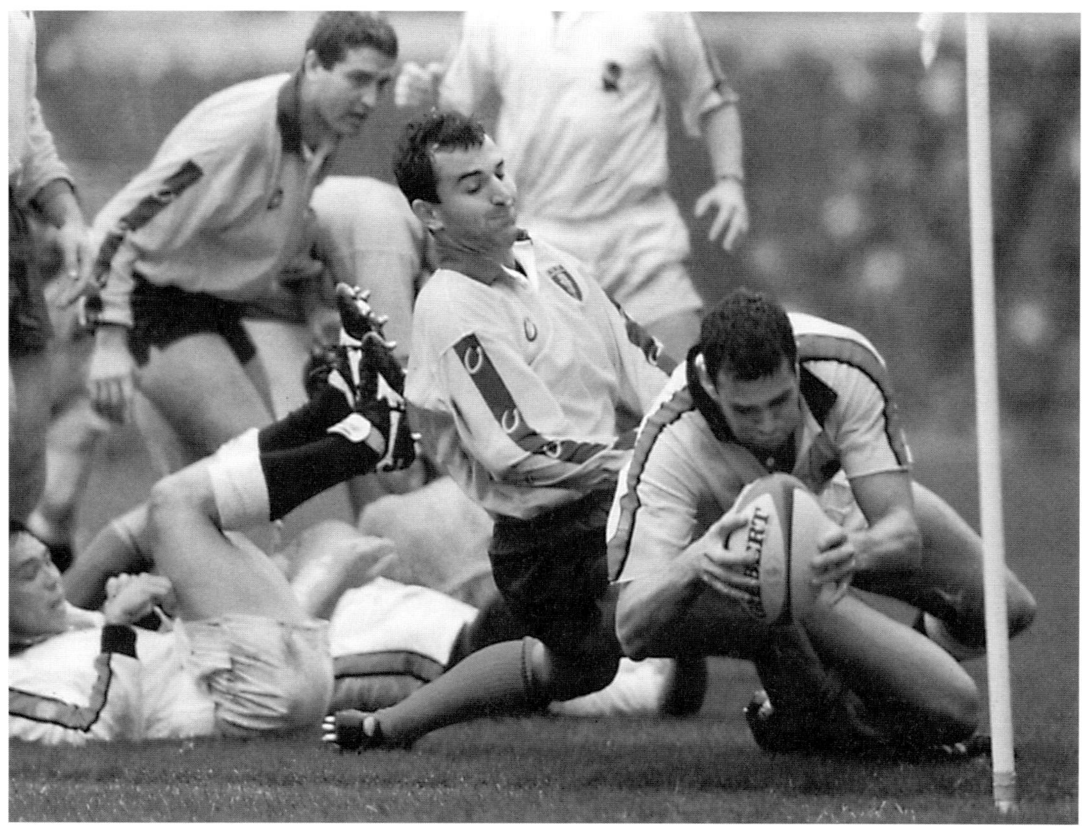

Martin Bayfield crosses the line against Romania. Unfortunately for the England lock, the try was disallowed. England went on to win the game 54–3.

November 1994 saw the arrival of a far more impressive touring team – Canterbury, the New Zealand Ranfurly Shield holders. They won all their eight games in England, only Bristol running them close (27–21), and the visit ended with a superb 44–20 victory at Treorchy. Among their players was the brilliant new All Black fly-half Andrew Mehrtens and the experienced All Blacks Richard Loe, Mike Brewer and Shane Philpott.

Canada were meanwhile testing their World Cup possibles and came away from a tour of Europe with all six matches lost including internationals against England (60–19) and France (28–9). Later they returned to play Scotland at Murrayfield with no change in fortune as the home team ended a long run of failure with a 22–6 success in poor conditions. In December and January, Italy coped well with the English winter, trouncing Middlesex (50–3). The weather caused the cancellation of their fixture with Surrey before they moved north to lose narrowly to Scotland A (18–16).

The New Zealand scrum-half prises the ball away from his forwards during the Under-21 international against England at Northampton. England were the winners by 15–6.

Away from World Cup matters New Zealand sent their Under-21 side in November and December 1994 to play six matches in England and one in Wales, against Swansea, who were thrashed 41–11. In England they mostly found stout opposition and ended their visit with a defeat at the hands of England's Under-21 team (15–6), but their schoolboys were more successful early in 1995. The tough youngsters were too good for everyone and achieved seven wins out of seven with successes against Wales Youth (29–3), Wales Schools (42–6), Scotland Schools (19–7) and England Schools (23–12). Their outstanding player was full-back Matthew Carrington, who scored all their points against Scotland and looked a fine all-round prospect.

Australia Schools had been in the British Isles shortly before their Kiwi counterparts and for once did not have matters all their own way. Their eight matches produced six wins, a draw (against the South-West) and a sound defeat by an impressive England team (30–3). Their best result was a 27–3 rout of Ireland, but they were fortunate to survive their game against Scotland, winning 18–17 thanks to a late score.

The last serious tourists to these islands during the season were Romania A, who followed a narrow victory over a Midlands XV (26–23) with an embarrassing 97–14 loss to an understretched England Emerging Players side, and Northern Transvaal, who won five of their six matches in Ireland and England, losing, surprisingly, to Ulster (16–15) but winning comfortably enough against all others, including an Emerging England side in Bristol (19–3). Four of South Africa's subsequent World Cup party were among them including scrum-half Van der Westhuizen, flanker Kruger, No. 8 Richter and prop Hurter.

Subsequently touring activities switched to the southern hemisphere, with the exception of Scotland, whose World Cup party had a brief warm-up interlude in Spain in which they beat a Madrid XV and the national team by a massive 62–7. The country's A team spent two weeks during the World Cup in Zimbabwe, taking all four matches comfortably without looking spectacular, and one suspected that they were there with the purpose of keeping players fit in case any were called up for the World Cup squad further south.

England's A players went further afield and struggled, mainly because the opposition in Australia – South Australia and Victoria apart – is usually strong. They also suffered from a spate of injuries. Out of six games in Australia half were won and the others lost, although the last match produced a fine win over an Australian XV (27–19). England A ended their tour in Fiji, where the national XV were overwhelming 59–25 winners. Despite various traumas, several players enhanced their reputations, notably among- the forwards, where the mercurial Chris Sheasby shone on a regular basis.

Elsewhere other countries warmed up for the World Cup, though few of the unfancied sides did their morale any good. The Ivory Coast were crushed by provincial sides in South Africa, Argentina lost both Tests in Australia, Canada were thrashed by the All Blacks and Western Samoa went down heavily to the Springboks. The South Africans' heavy list of injuries after their 60–8 victory made them wonder whether such outings serve any useful purpose.

After the World Cup it will be back to normal – that is until the next global competition looms. Yet in view of the huge impending changes in the game it is difficult to say what will become the norm in the forthcoming seasons.

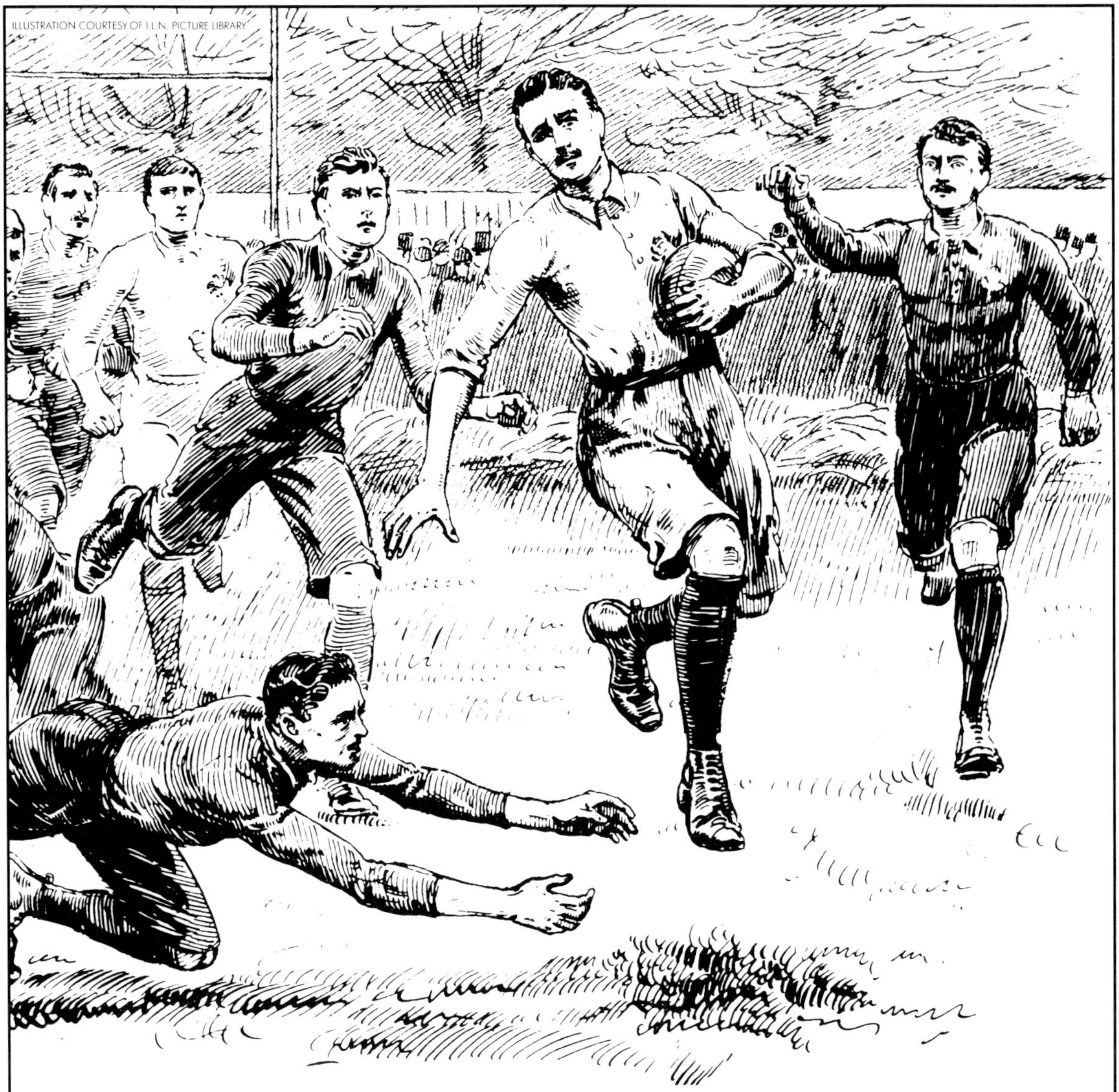

ILLUSTRATION COURTESY OF I.L.N. PICTURE LIBRARY

ALWAYS ONE TO SPOT A GOOD OPENING, ONCE ARCHIE HEARD ABOUT SAVE & PROSPER UNIT TRUSTS, THERE WAS NO STOPPING HIM

If you'd like to hear more about Save & Prosper Unit Trusts, just ring us on our free Moneyline: 0800 282 101. It could be just the break you need.

SAVE & PROSPER GROUP LTD IS A MEMBER OF IMRO AND LAUTRO

Refereeing the Modern Game

by Ed Morrison

Along with the game in general, refereeing has witnessed many changes. Not only in terms of the laws of the game, but also in the expectations of players, coaches, clubs and spectators alike. With the introduction of the Courage Leagues, additional pressures have been placed on referees. Results are all the more important: relegation can cost a club many thousands of pounds in lost sponsorship. For example, a club relegated from the Courage League Division 1 will automatically lose the Sky TV pay-out. Who, four or five years ago, could have envisaged club fixtures being shown live on television? Such is the profile the game of rugby football now enjoys.

With all the attendant pressures on players and referees, one might have expected there to be an increase in the incidence of foul play. Thankfully, this has not occurred, and players, referees and administrators deserve great credit for their efforts in cleaning up the game. Indeed, we are producing a sport with far less foul play. I share the opinion of many people in the game whose views I respect that rugby football today is far cleaner than at any time in its long history. This does not mean, of course, that we can rest on our laurels: our aim must be to eradicate foul play from rugby completely.

What has brought about this reduction in such incidents? Firstly, the players deserve praise for taking on board the responsibility afforded to them. Secondly, the introduction of touch-judges' intervention has had a remarkable effect. For many years at international level, touch-judges have had the power to intervene and report incidents of foul play to the match referee. Some four years ago, the Rugby Football Union, under Peter Brook's control, had the foresight to introduce 'active touch-judges'. These officials, many of whom were top-class referees in their own right, were appointed to Courage League games by the RFU. For the first time in our club rugby, incidents were to be reported to the referee as in internationals. This new development in itself had a remarkable effect on the behaviour of the players. It has taken me some time to come to terms with the frustration they feel when, in their opinion, touch-judges miss fouls.

In the near future I see the role of the touch-judges expanding further. The game has become so quick, almost impossible for one person to manage. The RFU has been experimenting in some Courage League matches by having the three match officials electronically 'wired up', thus allowing the touch-judges to pass on information such as offsides to the referee. This has had an enormous impact on matches. Defending players actually stay onside, allowing the ball-winning side space to work in. Thus the game becomes more free-flowing.

In recent times refereeing has come in for more than its fair share of criticism for not keeping pace with the modern game. In response the RFU

appointed their first national referees development officer. Steve Griffiths took up this role in the summer of 1993, with a brief to improve and develop refereeing skills throughout all levels of the game.

Wales were the first UK-based union to appoint an NRDO; Scotland followed suit soon afterwards, then England. More recently Ireland have named Owen Doyle as their NRDO. New Zealand were the first country to create the post many years ago, and now five of their provinces have referee development officers in place, each reporting to their NRDO. This expansion is designed to facilitate a more consistent approach to refereeing. How long before England follows the New Zealand lead?

One of the most significant changes in the modern game has been the attitude of the players towards their personal fitness. Gone are the days when you saw international rugby players drinking beer by the barrel. All players' fitness levels are closely monitored by Rex Hazeldine, the team's fitness advisor, and each player has his own personal schedule. A couple of years ago the referees sub-committee decided that referees should be no different. Now all RFU panel referees have to undergo two fitness tests per season. If anyone does not reach the accepted level, he can expect to receive no further RFU appointments until he regains the required standard. This, of course, means that referees, should they desire to carry on officiating at the top grade of the game, have to show the same commitment as the players they expect to control each Saturday of the season.

In early July at Trent College, a very significant meeting took place. Coaches from our national sides, the club coaches from the Courage League Divisions 1 and 2 and England's leading referees spent the weekend coming to a consensus on how the game should be refereed. It is hoped that everyone left Trent with a clear understanding and that we should now see a more consistent approach to refereeing. This consensus will go to all referee societies in England, from which the messages from Trent can then be cascaded to all levels. There will be follow-up meetings through the coming season: it is only through dialogue that this uniformity can be maintained.

The International Board has over the last year placed great emphasis on consistency in refereeing. The board has now in place a referees sub-committee whose aim is to achieve consistency on a worldwide scale. Over the past year, three conferences have taken place, in London, Sydney and Avion, France. Players, coaches and referees from many rugby-playing nations have made significant contributions to these conferences. The International Board, I believe, deserve great credit for their efforts to achieve what the players demand and are entitled to expect in terms of a consistent approach to refereeing.

As the game moves forward at a rapid pace, I hope that referees will accept the many challenges facing them and still find time to enjoy this marvellous game of rugby football.

THE NEXT LOGICAL STEP: A EUROPEAN CLUB SUPERLEAGUE?

BY CHRIS THAU

The attempt to launch a professional circus by signing on the top 900 players in the world has failed, and not only because it was a half-baked project. The chief cause of its downfall was the simple fact that the game was not ready for a takeover bid. The ethos of rugby football, a team game in which the individual, irrespective of his ability and box-office appeal, subordinates his energies to the collective effort, was too strong. The emergence of inspiring characters of the like of Jonah Lomu and the projected launch of a European club superleague may change all that, but at this stage in the history of the game people go to watch England against France rather than Carling against Sella, no matter how much the media try to boost the image of the individual at the expense of the unit.

Unquestionably, after the turmoil that engulfed rugby in the aftermath of the World Cup, the game is moving towards a period of adjustment in the so-called marketplace. Contracts are being signed; coaches and players are negotiating their pay packages. The unions sign the members of their national squads; the clubs follow suit. The next in line are the referees, team attendants – doctors, clubs secretaries, team managers, bar tenders, tea ladies etc. If the players are paid, so, they will say, should we be. A new character has also entered the scene: the agent. His role is to maximise the earnings of his clients – and himself, of course. Meanwhile the Packer circus greed has become legitimate, as the big clubs get stronger and the small clubs get weaker. Some will go under altogether.

However, in order to pay their players, the big clubs need additional revenue, and to create this they need to expand their horizons. In its present form, the market could be squeezed of a foreseeable future. An enterprising marketing agency from Scotland developed a proposal to map the way ahead, but the unions, alerted by the unholy coalition of players, agents, TV moguls and marketing agents pushing the project, vetoed it. They will handle it all themselves.

Once the Home Unions adopted the league system, perhaps unaware of its long-term implications, a European club competition became the next step. One wonders whether anything can be done to safeguard the game. Could the clock be turned back to the days before the advent of the

Leagues? Slavishly marketed as the ultimate solution to rugby achievement, league rugby has never been fully scrutinised. The traditional fixture lists of the senior English and Welsh clubs used to be the envy of the world. Perhaps the concept of a league championship is not as smart as it once appeared. Perhaps it places such intolerable pressure on players that it forces the game into the twilight zone of professionalism irrespective of what rugby really wants. Perhaps its suction effect, which has led to the formation of an elite at the expense of the majority of clubs, is not as healthy as was originally thought. Perhaps the maddening recruitment drives of the so-called ambitious clubs might raise another £2 to £3 million, but that will not suffice to meet the demands of the greedy brigade. The answer to this predicament is a European club competition, based on the model of the European Soccer Cup. Such a cup, or superleague, involving champion clubs and cup-winners from the Four Home Unions, France, Italy, Romania, Spain and the Netherlands is a perfectly feasible project. Television stations, mostly satellite but terrestrial, too, salivate every time the concept is mentioned.

The shape of things to come? Steve Bates makes a tackle in the Wasps game against Racing Club de France played back in 1990.

The idea is not new. In the 1960s FIRA ran a club competition modelled on the highly successful European Soccer Cup. Unfortunately, the gap in standards between the French and the Romanians on the one hand and the rest of the continental nations on the other was too wide to bridge. Throughout its four-to-five-year history, the final of the Nations Cup was regularly contested by the French and the Romanians. Among the winners were Béziers, Agen, Mont-de-Marsan, Grivita and Dinamo Bucharest.

The event was eventually abandoned, and in the 1970s an attempt to launch a club challenge between the French champions and the winners of the Welsh Merit Table was aborted due to the unacceptable level of violence of the encounters. Violence was also one of the reasons for the Nations Cup being ditched. A European club tournament was mooted in Wales a few years back, while some 20 years ago the season started with a four-way champions' tournament at Wembley.

In 1986 Toulouse organised the first Masters, a tournament involving clubs from the northern and southern hemispheres: Ponsonby from Auckland, Wests from Brisbane (then coached by Alex Evans), Banco Nacion from Argentina, L'Aquila from Italy, Toulouse and Agen from France and Farul Constanta from Romania. When Bath turned down their invitation, the organisers asked the Fijian Barbarians, touring Europe at the time, to replace the English. Toulouse, coached in those days by Pierre Villepreux and Jean-Claude Skrela, beat the Romanians in the final. The Masters was repeated in 1990 as the climax to Toulouse's centenary season, but the decision to invite national teams (Romania, Fiji and Russia), and provincial sides (Queensland and Wellington) as well as clubs (Bath and, obviously, Toulouse) diluted the concept.

In the 1990s the new 'ball game' promoted by an unholy alliance of media tycoons, TV executives, marketing agents, international players and power-hungry club officials could change, at least temporarily, the map of European rugby.

As long as the game at club level stays broadly amateur, the unions should be able to control the developments. But if rugby turns professional a continental club competition becomes inevitable. That could well be a blessing in disguise, in the sense that the breakaway group would relieve the immediate pressure on the game, and would probably do a disappearing act within four or five years of its launch, once 'market value' declines. While the project has strong commercial undertones and could in the long term undermine the power of the unions, it also has genuine sporting values. If a club strives to reach the top of the domestic hierarchy, it is equally commendable to attempt to become the best in the world or in Europe. The ambitions of a champion, be it an individual or a collective, cannot be artificially curtailed. From a sporting viewpoint as well as commercially, a club competition in Europe could be a winner.

Last year, the then president of Racing Club de France, Monsieur Labro, announced that the De Manoir Challenge, organised by RCF, would go international in 1995 and would involve top clubs from France, England, Wales, Ireland and Scotland. They felt that the time was ripe to play for higher stakes. They called their tournament the Euro Rugby Cup and the initial line-up, announced at a press conference in London, made impressive reading: Wasps, Swansea, Toulouse, Treviso, Blackrock,

Bath's Mike Catt finds a gap in the Garryowen defence to score a try, when the two sides met in September 1995.

Boroughmuir, with Cardiff, Orrell and Milan seemingly keen to be invited. M. Labro is no longer the president of Racing and consequently the De Manoir is likely to remain a French domestic competition for the foreseeable future. Toulouse, Swansea and Treviso pulled out, while the sponsorship deals failed to materialise. Certainly the Euro Rugby 1995 will be a very good tournament, but the big European club event has yet to be created. Undoubtedly the next project will be launched by the Five Nations themselves. Once England, Wales and Ireland are involved, the competition has genuine sporting value.

In the current rugby climate the arguments in favour of a European club tournament are compelling. Such an event will give domestic competitions greater scope and purpose. Unquestionably, a European Cup will create the missing dimension between international and domestic rugby, something coaches have been advocating for years. It would increase the profile of the game and ultimately lead to an improvement in the quality of European rugby. The success of its southern hemisphere equivalent, The Super-10, soon to become the Super-12, augurs well for such an event.

One of the by-products of the advent of European club football was the decline in popularity and eventual demise of the Four Home Unions Football Championship, historically the cradle of international soccer. Although rugby football has a different culture, it could suffer a similar fate. It is quite clear that, once unleashed, the market forces cannot be controlled. With the Five Nations increasingly seen as a two-horse race between England and France, a European club competition might endanger its prosperity and long-term viability, but, on the other hand, this Domesday scenario might not be realised after all. Perhaps the institution is stronger than we assume.

Matt Poole is stopped in his tracks by Italian international Paolo Vaccari during Leicester's pre-season clash against Milan in 1994.

THE BLEDISLOE CUP CENTENARY

BY CLEM THOMAS

The Bledisloe Cup is to Australia and New Zealand what the Calcutta Cup is to England and Scotland. On 29 July this year they celebrated, if not exactly its centenary – the cup itself did not come into being until 1931, when the huge trophy was donated by Lord Bledisloe, the governor-general of New Zealand – the 100th game between the two countries since 1903.

Coming so soon after their double failure in the World Cup, in which Australia, the holders, failed to get past the quarter-finals and New Zealand fell to their greatest adversaries, the Springboks (although most people would agree that the All Blacks looked the best team in the world), both sides had much to prove.

Two Tests were played on successive Saturdays and both qualified as Bledisloe Cup games, as usual. The first was played at Eden Park, Auckland, on 22 July. Australia astounded their supporters by dropping their most famed player, David Campese, who had made the greatest number of appearances in the series and who had scored most tries against the All Blacks, eight in all. His place went to Damian Smith. In addition, their record points-scoring Test player, the glorious Michael Lynagh, had retired after the World Cup and was replaced by the promising New South Walian Scott Bowen. The experienced lock Rod McCall was dropped for Warwick Waugh and Mark Hartill was brought in for Ewen McKenzie. Another major change was the introduction of the tough Steve Merrick at scrum-half for his first cap.

For their part, New Zealand trotted out their World Cup side and there was therefore little doubt as to who were the favourites.

Australia's Steve Merrick pressurises the All Black defence during the first match of the Bledisloe Cup at Eden Park, Auckland.

Like all these trans-Tasman affairs, it was a tremendously hard-fought battle on a cold, wet day in Auckland, and, although New Zealand won in the end by 28–16, Australia gave a terrific account of themselves and might well have won, but for an aberration of captaincy by Phil Kearns, who afterwards confessed that he had suffered a 'brain explosion'.

Having led at half-time by 10-6, the Wallabies were awarded a penalty by the Scottish referee, Ray Megson, with only about five minutes to go. Inexplicably, after Joe Roff declined the kick due to a loss of confidence, Kearns ordered a kick for touch instead of giving the job to John Eales, who has an accurate and mighty boot. A goal would have edged Australia ahead by 19–18; instead, a second dropped goal by Mehrtens and the conversion of a try by the irrepressible Lomu, scored after a fine break by Frank Bunce in the closing minutes, gave New Zealand a shaky win by a flattering margin. In addition to his conversion and two dropped goals, Mehrtens kicked five penalties. Australia scored a try through Willie Ofahengaue, converted by Roff, who also kicked two penalty goals to add to one from Matthew Burke.

Still it had been a great Test match, and as the All Black captain, Sean Fitzpatrick, admitted, 'Maybe at the end of the day we were lucky to win.' Bob Dwyer, the Australian coach, said: 'The scoreboard was disappointing, but the match wasn't.' Laurie Mains, the taciturn New Zealand coach, declared that: 'It was an outstanding Test match and both teams played exceedingly well.'

The Centenary Test itself was, alas, a far poorer match, not to mention a lesser spectacle, but by now the minds of the players were more tuned in to fiscal affairs than to rugby. Ross Turnbull, an ex-member of the Australian Rugby Union and the IB, along with ex-All Black Andy Haden, was touting the concept of a Kerry Packer World Rugby Championship, in competition to the Rupert Murdoch offer to the three southern hemisphere countries of in excess of $700 million over ten years. This new scenario threatened to split rugby globally, but in the end, it came to nothing, as Packer decided not to finance it. Nevertheless, many players became excited by the idea and were considering signing letters of intent, including the Australian captain, Phil Kearns.

Inevitably, this furore, which continued throughout the week before the Centenary Test, was a huge distraction and detracted much from the occasion. So it came as a relief when, after many past heroes of the Bledisloe Cup had been presented to the crowd and Sir Nicholas Shehadie, one-time lord mayor of Sydney and another great Wallaby ghost of the past, had handed over a crystal decanter to the retired Michael Lynagh, the game at last got underway. Fittingly, a bugler played the 'Last Post', seen by the conservative spectators, which most are, as the last rites for the amateur game as we have known it.

The crowd had somehow sensed the portents and seen the dark clouds that seemed to be gathering over their game and enthusiasm was seemingly hard to

Australia's Matt Burke beats All Black Jeff Wilson to the ball in the Centenary Test in Sydney.

come by. Perhaps the penny had dropped that they were supporting too many mercenaries who had but one thought, which did not include the good of the game or the lesser fry who have always supported them through thick and thin. After Australia had been substantially beaten by 34–23, Phil Harry, the Australian president, said: 'That sort of passionate performance between two countries, money cannot buy.' Phil Kearns responded by cryptically telling the crowd, 'We hope that whatever happens in the future, you will continue to support us.'

This time, the game barely lived up to its importance, and the result shielded many Wallaby deficiencies as the All Black backs found their World Cup form to score five superb tries, with guess who doing most of the damage. Yes, it was that man Lomu again. He upstaged every other player by setting up three tries and scoring one himself. Not in a lifetime in rugby going back over 50 years have I seen a phenomenon like him. Once he is into his stride, he not only has the power of a tank but the manoeuvrability of a hare. He has created a dynamic new verb, 'Lomued', which is what happened to Australia. For a 20-year-old, only two years out of school, he has a remarkable physique. In this centenary match, he wore a band on his wrist with a cross in the middle of a large S, signifying that he is a member of a Christian sportsmen's group.

This time the All Black forwards had done their homework and supplied a stream of ball to their backs, enabling centres Walter Little and Frank

Bunce to completely outplay Horan and Little. As well as Lomu's score, there were tries from Bunce (two), Mehrtens and Wilson with three conversions and a penalty goal coming from Mehrtens' boot. Australia's points came from tries by Smith and Ofahengaue and three penalties and a conversion by Burke.

In the third week of August, the threatened breakaway from the establishment petered out when Packer withdrew his support and all the Australian players signed contracts with the Australian Rugby Football Union. When Sean Fitzpatrick also signed with the New Zealand RFU, that revolt also crumbled, but not before both unions promised the players two places on their committee. They had tried to be emperors, but they had no clothes. It is now envisaged that provincial players will earn between $50,000 and $100,000 a year; Test players are to get between $100,000 and $200,000 and the occasional superstar player could earn up to $400,000.

Before our British players demand the same sort of money, they will have to earn it by consistently playing up to those southern hemisphere standards. They have a long way to go.

New Zealand captain Sean Fitzpatrick (centre) celebrates his side's Bledisloe Cup victory along with team-mates Jonah Lomu (left) and Jeff Wilson (right).

LOOKING BACK

Rugby's First Merit Table?

by Peter Watson

The following table, recording the events of the 1892–3 season, appeared in *The Football Annual* of 1893:

	Blackheath	O. Merchant Taylors	London Scottish	Oxford University	Cambridge University	Harlequins	Kensington	O. Leysians	Middlesex Wanderers	St Thomas's Hospital	Rosslyn Park	Guy's Hospital	Croydon	Clapham Rovers	Richmond
Blackheath	–	L	L	W/L	W/L	L	L	L	L	L	W	L	L	–	L/L
O. Merchant Taylors	W	–	D	L	L	L	W	W	–	L	L/D	L	L/L	L/L	–
London Scottish	W	D	–	D/W	L/W	L/D	L	L	L	L	L	–	–	L	L/L
Oxford University	L/W	W	D/L	–	D	L	W	L	L	L	L	–	L	–	L
Cambridge University	L/W	W	W/L	D	–	L	L	L	L	W	L	–	L	–	L/L
Harlequins	W	W	W/D	W	W	–	L	L	W/L	L	L	–	–	L	L/L
Kensington	W	L	W	L	W	W	–	D/W	W/D	D	D/L	L	L	L	–
O. Leysians	W	L	W	W	W	W	D/L	–	L	L	W/W	L	L	–	–
Middlesex Wanderers	W	–	W	W	W	W/L	D/L	W	–	–	L/L	L	W	–	L
St Thomas's Hospital	W	W	W	W	L	W	D	W	–	–	L	L	L	L	–
Rosslyn Park	L	W/D	W	W	W	W	D/W	L/L	W/W	W	–	W/L	D	L	W
Guy's Hospital	W	W	–	–	–	–	W	W	W	W	L/W	–	L	D	–
Croydon	W	W/W	–	W	W	–	W	W	L	W	D	W	–	D	–
Clapham Rovers	–	W/W	W	–	–	W	W	–	–	W	W	D	D	–	–
Richmond	W/W	–	W/W	W	W/W	W/W	–	–	W	–	L	–	–	–	–

The annual helpfully tells us to read each club's results from the top down, to see that, for example, Blackheath beat Old Merchant Taylors and London Scottish registered one loss and one win in their two games against each University, but lost to Rosslyn Park. Although not immediately recognisable as such, this was, in fact, a merit table. Today it would have been set out as follows:

	P	W	D	L	Pts	%
Blackheath	16	13	0	3	26	81.3
O. Merchant Taylors	15	10	2	3	22	73.3
London Scottish	16	10	3	3	23	71.9
Oxford University	14	9	2	3	20	71.4
Cambridge University	15	10	1	4	21	70.0
Harlequins	15	8	1	6	17	56.7
Kensington	16	6	4	6	16	50.0
O. Leysians	14	6	1	7	13	46.4
Middlesex Wanderers	14	6	1	7	13	46.4
St Thomas's Hospital	12	5	1	6	11	45.8
Rosslyn Park	19	5	3	11	13	34.2
Guy's Hospital	10	2	1	7	5	25.0
Croydon	12	1	2	9	4	16.7
Clapham Rovers	9	0	2	7	2	11.1
Richmond	11	1	0	10	2	9.1

The absence of leading provincial clubs from the table was due solely to the lack of fixtures with them and not to any implied superiority of the London or Oxbridge clubs. Yorkshire were champion county in seven of the eight seasons between 1889 and 1896. Of the 45 caps awarded in 1892–3, only 17 went to Metropolitan clubs (nine to Blackheath), and of the remainder, half (14) to players from Yorkshire clubs. Blackheath had regular fixtures with Manchester (from 1883) and Bradford (from 1886), and Richmond with Liverpool and Bradford (from 1887). There were occasional fixtures between other leading provincial clubs and those in the merit table, but not enough to warrant their inclusion. On the whole, clubs still played within a fairly restricted area close to their home grounds except for the odd tour further afield.

Of the London clubs not included, London Irish were not founded until 1898, but London Welsh, formed in 1885 and playing at Kensal Rise, had a number of fixtures with clubs in the table and must have been strong candidates for inclusion. Saracens (formed in 1876) had not built up their fixtures sufficiently to be considered and Wasps (formed in 1867) were described in their centenary history as being at a very low ebb at that time; indeed, they almost went out of existence.

Only two of the clubs – Blackheath and Richmond – still play where they started the 1882–3 season. Guy's moved from Raynes Park to Honor Oak Park during the season. The official opening of the new ground took place in January 1893. St Thomas's Hospital were based at Lambeth Palace

Birkenhead Park were one of a number of northern sides every bit as strong as those in the merit table. The England v Wales international (above) was played on their ground in 1894.

grounds until 1898, when they relocated to Chiswick. Harlequins were at their tenth ground in 20 years – Chiswick Park Cricket Club, where they remained from 1885 until 1897, giving themselves the chance to become a settled first-class side. London Scottish were at Old Deer Park, Richmond and Rosslyn Park at Gunnersbury Lane, Acton. Old Merchant Taylors were sharing with Old Leysians at Stamford Bridge. In 1894, London Scottish started their co-tenancy with Richmond, still in existence, at the Athletic Ground and Rosslyn Park and OMTs moved into Old Deer Park as co-tenants in their place. London Welsh did not arrive at Old Deer Park until 1957, when Park switched to Roehampton. OMTs had gone to Teddington in 1922, then to their present home at Croxley Green in 1937.

Oxford University were still playing at the Parks, staging occasional big matches at the nearby Merton College ground. They did not acquire Iffley Road until 1899. Cambridge moved at about the same time to Grange Road from Corpus Christi College ground.

The five clubs included in the table which are no longer in existence are:

Kensington Formed: 1873. Ground: Wood Lane, Wormwood Scrubs. Colours: Red and white. Described in *Football – The Rugby Union Game*, edited by Rev. F. Marshall (1892), as 'a stopping, not a scoring team who played a thorough forward game'. They disbanded in 1905. The leading player, Herbert Sibree, joined Harlequins and played scrum-half to the legendary Adrian Stoop. Sibree was capped three times for England in 1908 and 1909.

Old Leysians Formed: 1877. Ground: Stamford Bridge. Colours: Blue and white hoops. The old boys of the Leys School, established as a Methodist foundation in 1875. They were never a large school, but their old boys XV – one of the earliest formed – soon built up a phenomenal record against the leading clubs of the day. One of the reasons for their

Smile, please. Jeremy Guscott confronts the media after completing his first match following a year's absence from the game.

Lift-off for Martin Johnson during the top-of-the-table battle between Leicester and Bath. Leicester's win virtually ensured the end of Bath's monopoly on the League Championship.

Brian Moore prepares to take on his England colleague Steve Ojomoh during Harlequins' Pilkington Cup semi-final against Bath.

The charge of Pontypridd's Greg Prosser is checked by Cardiff's Chris John.

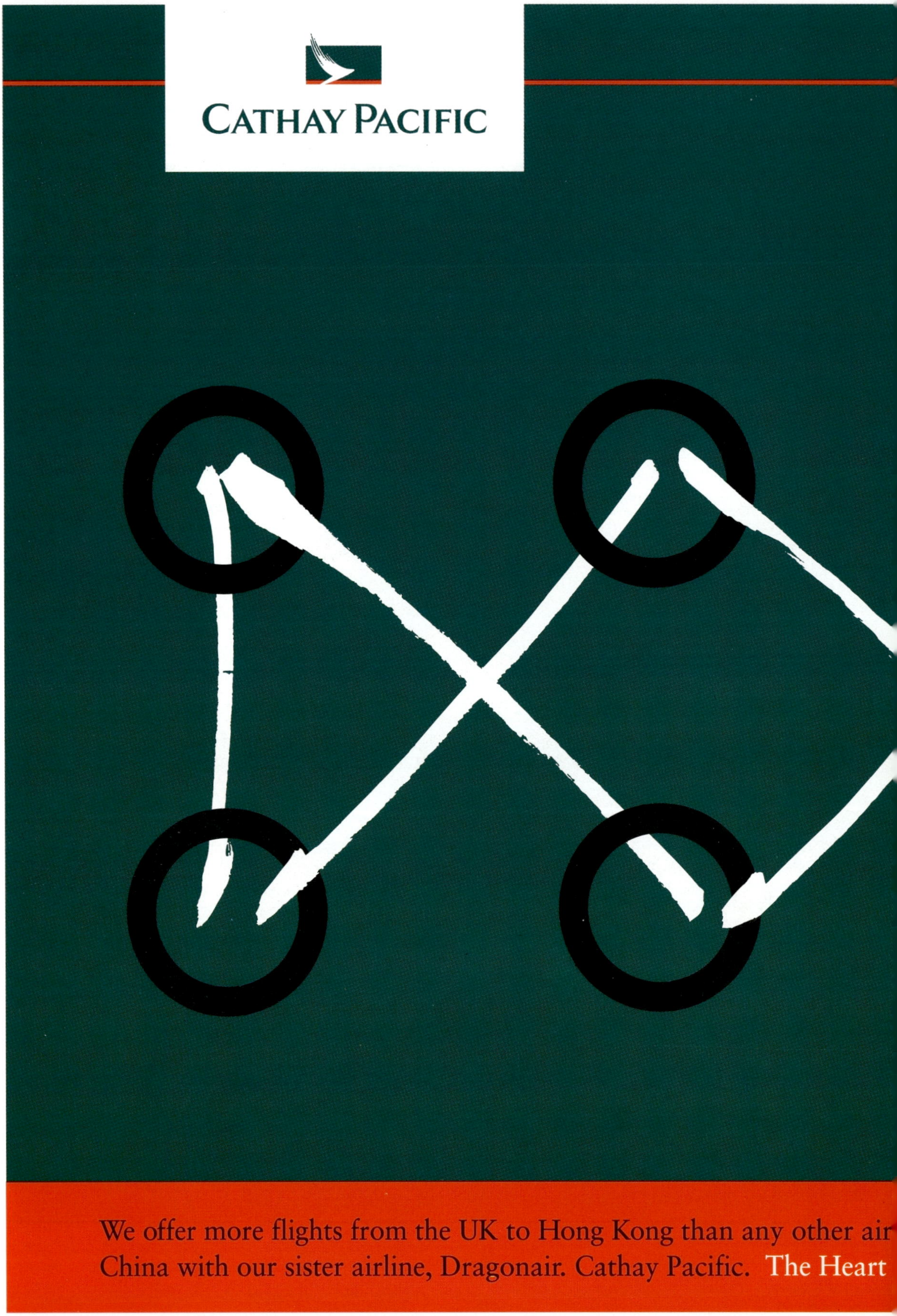

We offer more flights from the UK to Hong Kong than any other air
China with our sister airline, Dragonair. Cathay Pacific. The Heart

CONNECTIONS

...s well as the best connections around Asia and also on to 15 cities in

...a.

Tim Rodber powers towards the Romanian line during England's first home international of the season. Rob Andrew and Jeremy Guscott follow in close support.

Olivier Roumat gets a helping hand from his team-mates to win line-out ball for France during the 10–31 defeat by England at Twickenham.

South Africa's
Mark Andrews
beats Ian Jones to
the ball during
the match which
South Africa lost
15–23 to the
Barbarians at
Lansdowne Road.

MEANZ

WE ALSO HAVE A PASSION FOR FOOTSIE

We know our way around the FT-SE index and the stock market like others know their way around the rugby pitch. In fact, in the investment field, few are a match for Save & Prosper.

To find out how Save & Prosper can help with your savings and investment plans, call us free on 0800 282 101.

THE INVESTMENT HOUSE
SPONSORS OF ENGLISH RUGBY

UNIT TRUSTS · PEPS · PENSIONS · BANKING SERVICES

SAVE & PROSPER GROUP ONLY MARKETS ITS OWN PRODUCTS AND IS REGULATED BY THE PERSONAL INVESTMENT AUTHORITY AND IMRO.

success and for that of the school XV may have been the high proportion of matches they played against college teams in their home city of Cambridge. A fairly strong fixture list was maintained in the inter-war years, but sadly the full London list had to be discontinued in 1950, and since 1960 only the school is played on a regular basis.

Middlesex Wanderers Formed: 1874 (as Victoria). Ground: Richmond Athletic Ground. Colours: Black and orange. Wanderers, another club founded by Old Rugbeians, changed their name in the 1881–2 season. Marshall described them in 1892 as having had a 'fairly successful career but not an even one'. They produced two England internationals – Edwin Field at full-back (two caps in 1893), and threequarter Charles Hooper (three caps in 1894). Wanderers disbanded in 1896 and many of their members, including Hooper (who eventually became their captain) joined their co-tenants, Richmond, whose previously dire results showed immediate improvement. Some ex-Wanderers also joined Rosslyn Park.

Croydon Formed: 1875. Ground: Whitehorse Road, West Croydon. Colours: Lincoln green. Croydon, originally known as North Park, were not an outstandingly successful club and produced no international players. Apart from London club fixtures, they met Bedford, Leicester and Northampton in the late 1890s. They disbanded in 1903.

Clapham Rovers Formed: 1869. Ground: Wandsworth Common. Colours: Cerise and French grey. Rovers were not the only club formed in the 19th century to play rugby and Association football, but they were unique in the high standards they reached in both codes. Their soccer team won the FA Cup in 1879–80, having been losing finalists the previous season. They were founder members of the Rugby Union and

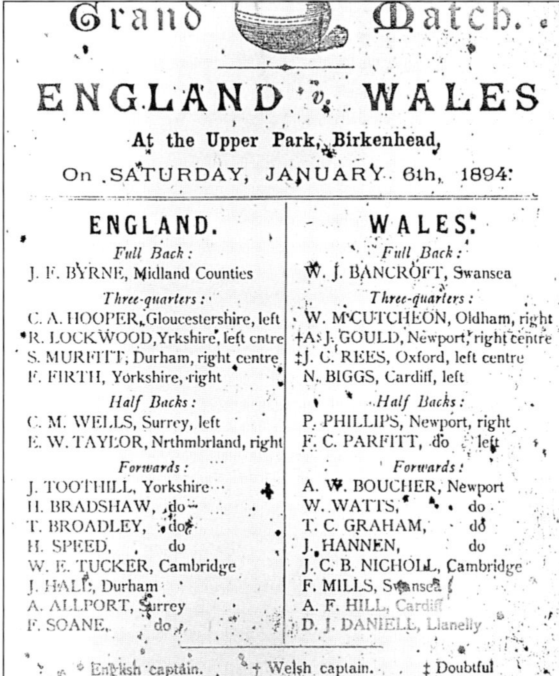

ENGLAND.	WALES.
Full Back :	*Full Back :*
J. F. BYRNE, Midland Counties	W. J. BANCROFT, Swansea
Three-quarters :	*Three-quarters :*
C. A. HOOPER, Gloucestershire, left	W. M'CUTCHEON, Oldham, right
*R. LOCKWOOD, Yrkshire, left cntre	†A. J. GOULD, Newport, right centre
S. MURFITT, Durham, right centre	‡J. C. REES, Oxford, left centre
F. FIRTH, Yorkshire, right	N. BIGGS, Cardiff, left
Half Backs :	*Half Backs :*
C. M. WELLS, Surrey, left	P. PHILLIPS, Newport, right
E. W. TAYLOR, Nrthmbrland, right	F. C. PARFITT, do left
Forwards :	*Forwards :*
J. TOOTHILL, Yorkshire	A. W. BOUCHER, Newport
H. BRADSHAW, do	W. WATTS, do
T. BROADLEY, do	T. C. GRAHAM, do
H. SPEED, do	J. HANNEN, do
W. E. TUCKER, Cambridge	J. C. B. NICHOLL, Cambridge
J. HALL, Durham	F. MILLS, Swansea
A. ALLPORT, Surrey	A. F. HILL, Cardiff
F. SOANE, do	D. J. DANIELL, Llanelly

* English captain.   † Welsh captain.   ‡ Doubtful

The team-sheet for England's match against Wales on 6 January 1894, featuring Charles Hooper of Middlesex Wanderers.

their rugby team, soon considered to be a leading club in the capital, produced four international players. These were two sets of brothers, all capped in the 1870s. Reginald Birkett (a threequarter) won four caps and scored England's first-ever try. He was also a soccer international as a goalkeeper, one of only three dual football internationals. His brother Louis (full-back), won three caps between 1906 and 1912. The other brothers were Charles (two caps) and Henry Bryden (one). They were both forwards and Henry was a notable runner. Rovers were disbanded in 1896.

The Rugby Football Annual, first published in 1913, also produced a merit table (shown below) based on southern clubs in the 1913–14 season. The only club omitted which was included in the 1892–3 table (apart from the four disbanded clubs) was St Thomas's Hospital. They had been the top hospital in the 1890s, having won the Hospitals' Cup nine times between 1888 and 1897. Guy's then took over, with the occasional interjection from the London. Newcomers were London Irish (formed in 1898), United Services (1882), Old Alleynians (1898), London Welsh (1885) and London Hospital (1865).

	P	W	D	L	F	A	%
Blackheath	18	14	1	3	328	94	80.6
Harlequins	18	14	1	3	304	119	80.6
Cambridge University	16	12	0	4	332	189	75.0
London Irish	10	6	1	3	100	75	65.0
Oxford University	15	9	1	5	180	173	63.3
O. Merchant Taylors	14	7	2	5	158	81	57.1
United Services	19	10	0	9	241	226	52.6
Richmond	16	7	1	8	193	246	43.7
Rosslyn Park	17	7	0	10	168	203	41.1
O. Leysians	13	3	2	8	95	188	30.7
Guy's Hospital	12	3	1	8	83	158	29.1
O. Alleynians	12	3	1	8	97	194	29.1
London Welsh	11	2	2	7	58	158	27.2
London Scottish	17	4	1	12	142	244	26.4
London Hospital	12	2	0	10	78	205	16.6

The Rugby Union finally gave their blessing to merit tables in 1976–7, when four regional tables were established as a run-in to the full Leagues 11 years later. The first winners were London Irish, Moseley, Gloucester and Gosforth.

25 Years Ago
from the pages of *Rugby World*

compiled by Nigel Starmer-Smith

January 1971

Rugby begins its big build-up in this month of January. The international programme makes a start, with Wales playing England in Cardiff and France meeting Scotland in Paris on 16 January, followed by Ireland v France in Dublin on 30 January.

From then until the end of March there is an international match most weekends, after which come the RFU presidential matches, in April, to round off the centenary celebrations.

With the greatest players in the world, from New Zealand, South Africa, Australia and France, being included in the president's team, it promises to be a memorable climax to the season. The names of men like Colin Meads, Brian Lochore, Dawie de Villiers and the new 'discoveries', Bryan Williams, the New Zealand wing, and 'Joggie' Jansen, the South African centre, make one wet the lips in anticipation. One only hopes they will all be able to make the trip.

And hardly are the presidential matches over than the Lions will be off to Australia and New Zealand on 6 May, to face up to the formidable men 'down under'. So the Lions' selectors, too, are faced with serious business.

More immediately we are concerned with the prospects for the home international season. France and Wales shared the title last time, and it could well be that the outcome will once again rest on the meeting between the two countries in Paris on 27 March – the last fixture of this season's Championship.

Vivian Jenkins – Editorial

No few than ten members of the England Under-25 side that beat the Fijians at Twickenham on 14 November were from Midlands sides, which would seem to suggest that the future of the game is assured in what has always been regarded as one of its strongholds.

Coventry provided full-back Peter Rossborough, centre David Duckham, lock Barry Ninnes and flanker Roger Creed. Bedford were represented by wing Jeremy Janion and scrum-half 'Jacko' Page (of Cambridge University). Loughborough Colleges provided prop Frank (*sic*) Cotton (from Lancashire) and hooker John Gray (also a member of Coventry). Leicester produced the No. 8, Gary Adey, and Northampton had fly-half Ian Wright. In addition, two other Midlands players, hooker Peter Wheeler of Leicester and flanker Peter Watts of Rugby, were among the reserves.

When Gareth Edwards, Cardiff and Wales scrum-half, gets injured and is away from rugby for a spell, he very often tests the injury by playing soccer.

Against the Fijians in October, when appearing for the Barbarians, Edwards hurt his right knee and was out of action for a time.

A fortnight after the injury, however, he tested out his knee by playing soccer for a village team in the Swansea valley, Gwaun-cae-Gurwen. He scored six goals!

Forwards usually take a long time to mature, but an exception to the rule is Llanelli's Derek Quinnell, who, at 21, has played in three positions for the club – lock, No. 8, and wing forward.

Derek Quinnell surfaces for air during Llanelli's game against Moseley at Stradey Park.

Which position does he prefer? 'In the second row,' he told me, 'because there I feel I can participate more freely. One has to specialise, even though forwards are now expected to do so many things, but I enjoy playing to such an extent that even if I was at scrum-half, I would probably be excited!'

This is typical of rugby players in west Wales, especially in Llanelli.

Quinnell is an excellent example of the way young players proceed up the rugby ladder in Wales. He attended Coleshill Secondary Modern School, Llanelli, and developed with Llanelli Schoolboys (Under-15 Group). He was kept out of the Welsh Schools XV by Allan Martin, now captain of Cardiff College of Education, who turns out for Aberavon on his vacations.

J.G.B. Thomas

February 1971

A bone of contention – and an excellent subject for discussion while downing a pint or two in the clubhouse – is the question of more competitive rugby in the form of leagues or knock-out competitions, Undoubtedly the urge stems from a shortage of money in the major clubs.

Rocketing costs, falling gates, lower bar takings, smaller profits from the 'swindles' and a reluctance by members to accept subscriptions at a more realistic figure, have prompted treasurers to issue dire warnings of disaster to club committees.

Amateur rugby, under that mild hypocritical influence for which the British are entirely misjudged abroad, is in the process of convincing itself that the game needs a new playing image and a more competitive spirit. To one who has spent a lifetime in Welsh rugby, that is, of course sick humour. However, the clarion call has a truer amateur ring about it if the theoretical motive is the improved standard of rugby, and not simply a base profit move.

In the final analysis, the overriding factor which governs the control of rugby must be the pleasure of the players. We must never allow the course of the game at higher levels to become too arduous for the true amateur doing an ordinary job of work.

The playing development of rugby must never be decided by the spectator or the treasurer. The ideas outlined here of competitive rugby and sponsorship, however, need not clash with the true object of our game.

Wilf Wooller

When we all go decimal and metric what will the Rugby Union do about renaming the 25-yard line? The matter will be discussed by the International Board at its meeting in London in April.

RU secretary Robin Prescott says: 'Why not call it the "quarter line"?' Why not, indeed – that's much better than the 22.860-metre line!

Over the last ten years Ireland have beaten

France only once. Ireland's solitary success came at Lansdowne Road just two years ago, which must make for added interest in the Tricolours' visit to Dublin on 30 January.

Since last season, the Irish have completed a short tour to Argentina, and we can only hope that the results from South America are not reflected in the Championship table at the end of the 1971 campaign.

The Inter-Provincial competition finished in Belfast in December, with Ulster retaining their title following a 6–3 home win over Leinster. It was a result that owed everything to team captain and out-half Mike Gibson, who kicked the penalty goal and later dropped the goal that beat Leinster in the second half.

Leinster had not the strength behind the scrum to match the shining brilliance of Gibson or the efficiency of centre Harry Rea, a former cap, and Dick Milliken, a new name from Queen's University who should achieve international recognition before very long.

Peter McMullen

Andy Ripley says he is, and he certainly strikes me as a man who does not take decisions lightly, or attempt anything without thorough preparation. The manner in which he has steered his own education shows that. For his age, his experience is wide.

Two years ago he spent four months hitch-hiking through the United States and Mexico. He went with the £50 allowance, and when that ran out, as it soon did, he worked.

Sometimes he slept in ditches, sometimes he travelled in aeroplanes and lived in hotels, but he kept going and doing a wide variety of jobs. Painting the chalets at a ski resort he found the most lucrative, and lived in fine style. His most interesting job was on a dude ranch in the Rockies.

'Can you ride?' I asked him.

'Yes, but badly,' he said. 'Anyway, I was the washer-up and general handyman.'

He travelled thousands of miles, met hundreds of people of all types, learned the hard facts of economics, the value of money. He was 30.

In another year he hitch-hiked to Greece and Turkey and for two months lay on beaches in the sun.

Ripley came down from university the summer before last with a degree in economics, and decided that the next stage of his education should be with a firm of accountants in London, to whom he is articled.

So now he lives in Islington, and is by this time qualified to play for Middlesex, which the county selectors know. I should not be surprised if they take advantage of it.

It seems to me that young Ripley will go far. 'Any game I take up I want to play well, and I realise that to do so in rugby now, one must be dedicated,' he told me. That, I believe, is all he must be to 'go places'.

Rupert Cherry

March 1971

The most dramatic match I have ever introduced on television was the Barbarians versus Brian Lochore's All Blacks at

Andy Ripley in action for Rosslyn Park at the Middlesex Sevens.

Twickenham in 1967. I doubt very much if in my lifetime there will ever be a more nerve-shattering couple of minutes' play than when the New Zealanders fought their way out of a situation of certain defeat with two spectacular tries to win 11–6.

My most surprising TV match also involved the Barbarians, at Gosforth last October, when the Fijians ran riot against the pick of British rugby talent, which on the day suffered, it seemed to me, from an overdose of complacency.

The most memorable tackle was also in a Barbarians match, against the Springboks, when, at Cardiff Arms Park in 1961, Haydn Mainwaring crushed South Africa's captain, Avril Malan.

The most frustrating commentary was at Cape Town, when Tom Kiernan's Lions should have beaten South Africa in the Third Test, on 13 July 1968.

The most efficient – indeed, the best – teams I have watched were the 1951 Springboks, captained by Basil Kenyon and the 1967 All Blacks in Britain, coached by Fred Allen.

For personal delight, Richard Sharp's solo try against Scotland at Twickenham in 1963 tops the list, and the best forward I have watched is Ken Goodall of Ireland, who, unhappily for the Union game, has departed to the Rugby League, where he has already been a tremendous success.

My favourite interview was with Tom Kiernan last year, on the day he played in his 47th international match for Ireland, and the most memorable quote came from Scotland's hooker Frank Laidlaw, who said: 'When I lose a strike on our own put-in, it's like a personal bereavement.'

My personal wish, in television terms, is that we never lose sight of the fact that rugby is only a game.
Cliff Morgan

'I was 21,' observed Nairn MacEwan wryly, 'when the press first referred to me as a veteran!' An exaggerated widow's peak had developed soon after leaving school, and to many of the Fourth Estate – as one knows to one's cost – thinning hair is regarded as no less accurate a guide to age than teeth in a horse.

Certainly, all rugby players whose partings, in Albert Morris's apposite quip, are now such sweet sorrow, will sympathise with the 29-year-old MacEwan, who is more than tired of being congratulated, in all sincerity, on his remarkable form 'for a man of 35...'

However, MacEwan has not yet been driven to a similar defence to that of the much-feared London Scottish tight-head prop Robin Challis, who now carries his marine documentation to prove that he occurred no earlier than 1937, though, as I have noted before, his exact antiquity is as heatedly debated as that of some newly uncovered fossil.
Norman Mair

The Welsh Secondary Schools have served notice on the English Schools (19 Group) and the French Schoolboys, both of whom they are to meet in April, that they are again a powerful force. Last season Wales won all four matches at this level, beating England 6–5, France 16–3, Scotland 21–0 and Yorkshire 25–6.

This season's Welsh Secondary Schools XV started their international campaign with a match at Llanelli on 2 January against the Scottish Schools.

Their three players remaining from last year's XV were all forwards, J. Hardman (Neath GS), R. Thomas (Llandeilo County Sec.) and S. Lane (Tredegar Comp.), but their backs proved to be well up to the usual high standard. They beat Scotland with some ease, winning 30–6, and doing much as they liked in the later stages.
Geoff Abbott

Judging by reports which have been

reaching New Zealand, there seems to be some concern whether the 1971 Lions will be strong enough to defeat the All Blacks in the coming tour. By rights, there should also be reports going the other way that there are genuine fears that the All Blacks, especially among the backs, will be able to foot it with leading Lions candidates.

Freddy Allen, the former All Blacks coach, was the first to sound this warning when he visited England on his way home from seeing part of the All Blacks' tour of South Africa. 'Beware the Lions,' was Allen's message.

Allen told me that, compared with his experiences with the 1967 All Blacks, British Isles rugby was being based on much firmer grounds.

In his opinion, he felt that the Lions' management of Dr Doug Smith and Mr Carwyn James would have little trouble in welding the players of the Four Home Unions into a fine team.

The names of the talented English centres, David Duckham and John Spencer, are already becoming household words in New Zealand, and there has been great interest, too, in the news that Gareth Edwards and Barry John are leading candidates for the half-back positions, though neither quite lived up to their pre-

tour billing when Wales came to New Zealand in 1969.

One Welshman who did impress New Zealanders was John Dawes, the centre, and any back line that can call on Edwards, John, Dawes, Duckham and Spencer – plus John Williams at full-back – is regarded by New Zealand as highly dangerous.

In the meantime, New Zealand have been having some worries about their own back-line strength.

Grahame Thorne is now in South Africa, Earle Kirton has retired, and Chris Laidlaw is back at Oxford – so this means that New Zealand will have to reform their back line minus Thorne, Laidlaw and Kirton.

Sid Going, provided his knee injury heals, is now the number one scrum-half, but it is anyone's guess who will be his partner.

There are worries, too, about Bryan Williams, the dashing young goal-kicking wing who was the find of the South African tour. Since returning home, Williams has had several very tempting offers to play Rugby League in England.

April 1971

To the delight of the whole rugby world, 'Bill' Ramsay, one of the game's most able administrators, was honoured at the New Year, becoming the first knight of rugby football. Sir William is known and respected not only in England, for he has done so much for the promotion of friendship and goodwill amongst the rugby-playing nations of the world.

The Rugby Football Union rejoices at the honour given to its centenary president.
RFU Statement

John Bevan follows many former Cardiff College of Education students who have been capped, including Dewi Bebb, Clive Rowlands, David Nash, John Lloyd, Gareth Edwards and Brian Price. The last-named went back for a year's special course; and the senior PE lecturer at the College, Roy Bish,

Barry John's performances in New Zealand helped the British Lions to a famous 2–1 series victory

has coached Cardiff and Oxford University with success.

The season's first XV captain, Allan Martin, from Aberavon, played for the Welsh Under-25 side against the Fijians.

Bevan is essentially a product of coaching, and he owes much to the fact that many people have guided him along the path that led to the national XV. He still has much to learn, of course, especially in positional defence, but this will come with experience.

'Wise coaching is invaluable,' says Bevan, 'especially for a younger player. At college, Leighton Davies has charge, while Clive Rowlands coaches the Welsh XV. They will tell you where you went wrong in a match or in practice. I feel that the correcting of faults is far more important to a young player than a shower of praise.'
J.B.G. Thomas

Men other than Herioters have played full-back for Scotland – but the practice would appear to be dying out. Ian Smith, who directly followed Colin Blaikie, is the seventh Scottish full-back out of Goldenacre. In the post-war era alone, besides Smith and Blaikie, we have had Tommy Gray, Ian Thomson and Ken Scotland.

The eighth is waiting in the wings – or, to be more precise, on the right extremity of the Heriot's threequarter line, since the aforesaid Colin Blaikie is still holding down the full-back berth. However, when, like Andy Irvine, you are still only in your first year out of school and a mere 19 years of age, time is hardly yet the enemy.

On the right wing in the Gillespie's XI who won the Craigour League in primary schools football, Irvine had played no rugby before, at the age of 12, he moved on to Heriot's. Three seasons in the school first XV and skipper in his last year, he captained the Edinburgh Schools XV who won all their matches in his second year in the

district side.

And in 1969 and 1970 he was capped by the Scottish Schools, easily their most memorable result being the 17–0 defeat of the Sassenachs on his own familiar Goldenacre.
Norman Mair

On the morning of the Scotland v Wales match, Hawick referee Barrie Laidlaw, who, with Gala's Bob Burrell, retires at the end of this season, was involved in an amusing incident while controlling the Selkirk v Ayr clash.

Late in the game he was knocked over by Ayr second-row forward Les McCall, and Mr Laidlaw found himself having to control the match from the bottom of a loose ruck. Despite the crowds and the players' enjoyment of this incident, Mr Laidlaw was still able to blow his whistle to halt the game.

May 1971

It has been observed in some quarters – with a certain amount of reservation, I feel – that this is the first time a Welshman has ever captained a Lions team on tour. Well, no Lions team has ever won a Test series either, so perhaps Dawes can turn the tide. If he fails, he will be in good company!

I have a hunch that his team may be better than many expect. Behind the scrum, certainly, they could rise to great heights if the luck runs their way.

Dr Doug Smith, himself a former Lion, has the experience and know-how to make an excellent manager, and the presence of a doctor in the party is always a bonus point. Carwyn James, the assistant manager and coach, was a highly skilled performer at fly-half for Wales, and has all sorts of ideas for developing new attacking methods behind the scrum. Perhaps this team will show New Zealand something, instead of only learning.
Vivian Jenkins

Kirton thought the Lions would be at a disadvantage through not having enough forwards who were both big and mobile. This particularly applied to props and flankers. Some of Wales' best forwards took a hammering when they went to New Zealand in 1969, he said, and this was largely due to the fact that there were not enough big 'uns.

Of course, size has gone up in the last few years; 6ft or 6ft 1in is reckoned small for the back row now.

Kirton added: 'So far as the second row is concerned, the disadvantage may not be so great. There is a scarcity of top-class second-row men in most countries, and this could include New Zealand, especially if Meads does not play.'

Of the forwards he had seen playing this year, Kirton thought the most likely man to succeed in New Zealand was Peter Dixon. Of course, Kirton has had a good view of Dixon, having played behind him in the Harlequins side, but he assured me he did not say this simply because they were in the same club. Dixon is 6ft 3ins and weighs 15st 2lb, which is a fair enough size for a No. 8, and he has the advantage of having learned a lot of his rugby from a New Zealander, John Baird, at Oxford.

Behind the scrum, Kirton thought the Lions might be better off than New Zealand, although they would lack strength on the wings. This might affect the style of play they would have to adopt.
Earle Kirton talking to Rupert Cherry

The rugby is serious, as it should be, and you won't find a New Zealander smiling when he is playing. Perhaps it is a second religion to them – and who am I, a mere Welshman, to criticise their approach!

New Zealanders are proud, sensitive people and extremely generous, and this generosity has no limits in rugby football. Nothing will be too good for the Lions.

They will be amazed at the reception they will receive in Auckland on Sunday 16 May, for there will be about 5,000 at the airport to greet them. After that, the Lions will never be out of the public eye, except when in bed, and their lives will be the talk of New Zealand. Every paper in every town visited will carry pictures of the team, arriving, walking, training, shopping, eating, dancing, drinking, talking, and, of course, in action on the field.
J.G.B. Thomas

A year ago, 6ft 3in, 15½st Geoff Wheel was playing soccer as a centre-half in Swansea City's Welsh League side. Now he has switched to rugby and is establishing himself as a lock with Swansea.

Wheel's conversion began last close season, when, after a friendly discussion at work over the merits of the two games, he was invited to sample rugby training with Mumbles, a local Swansea club.

Geoff Wheel, Swansea's 6ft 3in lock forward.

'I thoroughly enjoyed it,' he said. 'What's more, I enjoyed just as much the rugby atmosphere.'

Since then, 19-year-old Wheel hasn't looked back. He moved to Swansea, made his first-class debut at Christmas, and is now one of the club's three lock fowards.

Here are my top 15 schools in Britain for

1970–1 (in alphabetical order within their countries):
England – Clifton, Harrow, Millfield, Reigate GS, Roundhay and Uppingham.
Wales – Cardiff HS, Llandovery and Monmouth.
Scotland – Fettes, Royal High School and George Watson's.
Northern Ireland – Belfast Model, Campbell and Methodist College, Belfast.
G.W. Abbott

June 1971

The International Board's decision to experiment with raising the value of a try to four points has met with approval in some quarters, but I am afraid it does not appeal to me. The board has gone only halfway, in my opinion, and the experiment risks falling between two stools.

Admittedly, it will provide an added inducement for scoring tries, which is all to the good, as far as it goes. But the rewards may not be so big as at first sight they appear.
Vivian Jenkins

Quite the most pleasing point about England's team to tour the Far East is that 'Budge' Rogers has been appointed captain.

I like the look of the team that Rogers will have under his command, but it is tough luck on Chris Wardlow that he had to call off the Lions' trip to New Zealand because of his broken jaw. His tackling will certainly be missed 'down under', but Chris Rea, of Scotland, who takes his place, will provide compensatory speed off the mark in the centre.

The England party is: Full-back: P. Rossborough (Coventry); Threequarters: P. Glover (Bath), J. Janion (Bedford), R. Lloyd (Harlequins), C. Wardlow (Northampton), D. Roughley (Liverpool), R. Webb (Coventry); Fly-halves: R. Cowman (Loughborough Colls), J. Finlan (Moseley); Scrum-halves: N. Starmer-Smith; Forwards: F. Cotton (Loughborough

Colls.), J. Broderick (Coventry), C. Stevens (Harlequins), J. Gray (Loughborough Colls), P. Wheeler (Leicester), P. Larter (Northampton), C. Ralston (Richmond), R. Uttley (Northern), A. Neary (Broughton Park), D. Rogers (Bedford), R. Creed (Coventry), C. Hannaford (Bristol).
Vivian Jenkins

The major talking point in Scottish rugby, transcending even the record margin by which Scotland beat England in the centenary match in notching their second victory over the original enemy in eight days, is the SRU circular detailing the recommendations of the consultative committee set up to investigate the establishment of a system of competitive rugby in Scotland based on national leagues.

'Why was he born so beautiful? Why was he born at all?' That's what hundreds of rugby men chanted as Prince Philip rose to speak at the Rugby Union's Centenary Dinner at the Hilton Hotel, London, on 17 April, with Sir William Ramsey, the RFU president, in the chair.

Prince Philip grinned at this typically good-natured rugger reception from guests numbering over a thousand, including hundreds of international players, and then he brought the house down with a splendid speech.

Earlier, at 'Twickers', the Queen, accompanied by Prince Philip, had unveiled a centenary plaque at the West Stand and then met the President's Overseas XV and the England team prior to their match – the culminating encounter in a four-game series.

July 1971

It will not be long before we know how really good are the 1971 Lions. The first international against New Zealand takes place at Dunedin on 26 June, and the remaining three follow in fairly rapid succession – at Christchurch (10 July),

Wellington (31 July) and Auckland (14 August).

The chips are therefore down, and one can only wish John Dawes and his team the best of luck in their efforts. A winning series would give an immense boost to British rugby. The All Blacks and Springboks have held sway for so long that it is high time that Britain, which gave the game to the world, had a turn.

New Zealand, meanwhile, is not as happy as it might be about its rugby. The defeat in last year's series in South Africa was a chastening one, and for once New Zealanders are asking themselves whether their rugby is as good as it used to be.

The doubts are only relative, but at least it has shown that they are not unbeatable, and the Lions, to that extent, can take heart.

The retirement of Brian Lochore and other leading players has been said to improve the Lions' chances, but I am not so sure about that, because New Zealand rugby has such strength in depth and there are always new players coming on to replace the old.

Still, it is a new experience, going round the country, to hear New Zealanders expressing doubts about their own prospects.
Vivian Jenkins

Rugby World Player of the Year – Barry John. Runners-up – 2. Gareth Edwards, 3. Bob Hiller, 4. John Dawes, 5. Peter Brown.

Tony Neary, the Broughton Park and Lancashire flanker, is one of a particularly rare breed in having played for his country at 15, 19 and senior level – a feat previously achieved only by A.J. Herbert (Marling and Wasps), J.R.C. Young (Bishop Vesey's and Harlequins) and T.C. Wintle (Lydney GS and Northampton).

Young went one further than the others in that he toured with the Lions (in 1959).

Neary still harbours a keen desire to do likewise – a prospect which should not be beyond him, as he is still only 22.

Queensland (three penalty goals, two dropped goals) 15; Lions (goal, two penalty goals) 22 (Brisbane, 12 May).

There was hardly a roar from the Lions in this the first game of their tour, watched by a crowd of about 12,000. It was, indeed, a very plaintive beginning.

Admittedly, they arrived in Australia only 48 hours before the kick-off, after a 12,000-mile flight, but it still seemed incredible that a team whose individual talents were so advanced could put up such an ordinary performance.

August 1971
Lions rampant! This could be the only verdict after John Dawes' British Isles team roared through their first ten provincial games without prospect of defeat and devoured the All Blacks in the First Test.

The Lions' rugby, especially in the 47–9 demolition of Wellington, has been glorious, and they have set crowd records in almost every centre. Dawes has been tremendous as captain and the management of Dr Douglas Smith and Carwyn James splendid.

It has not been all plain sailing. The ugly match against Canterbury cost the Lions 'Sandy' Carmichael and pack leader Ray McLoughlin, who were replaced by 'Stack' Stevens and Geoff Evans. Yet this served only to stiffen their sinews for the First Test, which they won quite convincingly, even if their tactics were more austere than the Lions wished.

New Zealand expected the Lions backs to be superior and so it has proved, especially in the magical play and sensational goal-kicking of Barry John, the classical arts of Michael Gibson's midfield play and the pugnacious thrust of John Bevan on the wing.

What New Zealand did not expect was

that the Lions forwards would be so expert at scrummaging that provincial packers were tossed about like feathers and even the mighty All Blacks had to give ground.
Donald Cameron

Richard Sharp, the former England fly-half and captain, suggested in a recent speech that the England selectors should be replaced by one man – similar to soccer's Sir Alf Ramsey.

Barry John, whose scoring feats for the Lions have taken New Zealand by storm, confesses to at least one weakness.

'I wish I could make myself concentrate more,' he says. 'Whenever we're winning easily, I tend to lose interest and do silly things.'

That certainly applied in the Lions' match against Waikato, at Hamilton. Late in the second half, when the tourists were well on top, John got the ball somewhere near his own 25, with no Waikato man near him. Instead of kicking the ball to touch, or running, either of which he could have done easily, he stood stock-still, as though he were conducting a private debate about what to do next.

'Perhaps he's going for a stroll by the river,' said someone. Meanwhile, the Waikato forwards were bearing down on him full-tilt, and disaster seemed imminent. But John is such an instinctive evader that he dodged his way out of it somehow, and cleared the ball to touch. Still, it could have gone the other way.

It doesn't do to dawdle when New Zealand forwards are in the offing. It's comforting to know, though, that even a player of John's stature can have a weakness; and even more comforting to know that he is prepared to admit it. But his team-mates still call him 'King' John.

The status of Springbok rugby – newly enhanced by the victories last year over the All Blacks – was preserved in the short tour series against France, which reached its climax in Durban on 19 June.

That is to say, it was preserved statistically. On their nine-match tour, France lost once only, in the first international. They drew the second, and on balance it is fair to say that morally they were the victors on the day and should, at least, have shared the rubber.

September 1971
May I suggest that all future international matches – as in our own home Championship series – be controlled by neutral referees, probably drawn from France, South Africa and/or Australia. If their general behaviour on and off the field is anything to go by, there seems no reason why referees from Fiji should not also be considered.

It is, of course, not necessarily certain that a neutral referee will automatically do a better job than a local man, but an honest attempt to see that justice is done becomes apparent when players know that the official is of a nationality different from those of the teams involved.
R. Burman – reader's letter

The 1971 Springboks made the biggest-ever impact of any sporting team to visit Australia. Previously, Rugby Union had commanded little attention in Western Australia, South Australia and Victoria, where one out of every 100 residents of those states had never heard of the game, nor of a Springbok player.

Now all this has changed. Anti-apartheid feeling, vigorously stirred up by the Australian press, radio and TV, made Rugby Union and the Springboks top-line news daily throughout the length and breadth of Australia during the six-week tour.

The result of this massive publicity also proved a financial bonanza for Australian Rugby Union, and the game had its greatest financial boost in its near 100-year history.

Although somewhat overshadowed by his elder brother, Quintin Dunlop, the West of Scotland and Scotland hooker, Ayr prop Alan Dunlop recently proved himself no mean competitor.

During Ayr Rugby Club's annual golf outing, Alan, who had never been on a golf course in his life, achieved a hole in one on the Stranraer course.

He reached the turn in 70 and started back 8,6. At the 187-yard 12th, he took his 30-year-old hickory-shafted driver and thrashed a mighty shot right into the cup, to the amazement of the onlookers – and, of course, of Alan Dunlop.

There is not much rest for top rugby players these days. No sooner is the Lions' tour of Australia and New Zealand over – and what an arduous and exhausting tour it has been! – than the new home season, with all its challenges, looms up again.

For the sake of every Lion who took part in the energy-draining battles 'down under', I hope their clubs – and the individuals who take around those 'scratch' XVs in September and October – will spare them the embarrassment of having to refuse invitations to play in these early matches.

A man has only so much to give, and it is impossible for a player to keep in top pitch for 20 months on end. That is what it involves – eight months of a home season, followed by four months, or thereabouts, 'down under', and then eight months at home again.

Vivian Jenkins

October 1971

Barry John topped the Lions' scorers with 188 points, all but eight of them obtained in New Zealand. He easily eclipsed the previous Lions record in New Zealand of Malcolm Thomas (73 points on the 1950 tour). The 1971 Lions' scorers were:

	T	C	PG	DG	Pts
Barry John	6	31	28	8	188
Bob Hiller	2	25	16	2	110
John Bevan	18	–	–	–	54
David Duckham	11	–	–	–	33
Gerald Davies	10	–	–	–	30
Alastair Biggar	9	–	–	–	27
Mike Gibson	5	1	1	1	23
John Dawes	5	–	–	1	18
John Williams	2	2	1	1	16
John Spencer	4	–	–	–	12
John Taylor	4	–	–	–	12
Mervyn Davies	3	–	–	–	9
Gareth Edwards	3	–	–	–	9
Chris Rea	3	–	–	–	9
Peter Dixon	2	–	–	–	6
Arthur Lewis	2	–	–	–	6
'Sandy' Carmichael	1	–	–	–	3
Geoff Evans	1	–	–	–	3
Ray Hopkins	1	–	–	–	3
John MacLauchlan	1	–	–	–	3
Ray McLoughlin	1	–	–	–	3
Derek Quinnell	1	–	–	–	3

Despite all the tensions created by the anti-apartheid demonstrations, South Africa's 1971 tourists made a clean sweep in Australia, winning all 13 games and scoring

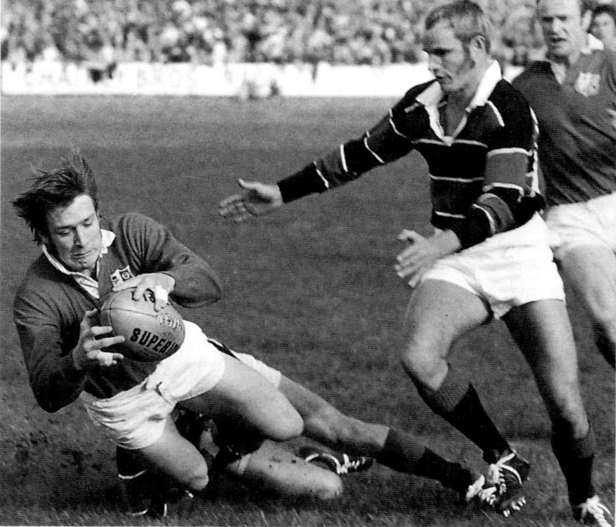

John Bevan scores the Lions' first try against Wanganui–King Country during his side's impressive 22–9 victory.

396 points against 102. They were never fully extended, even in the internationals, which they won 19–11, 14–6 and 18–6.
To his credit, 'Sandy' Carmichael, the Scotland and Lions prop, will tell no tales of Canterbury. The mess his face was in – and the photograph taken of his battered countenance merited an X certificate – was accentuated by the fact that the opposite eye to that ravaged in the Canterbury game at Christchurch had the scars of six stitches, necessitated by an accident in training when he collided with Derek Quinnell.

The injury that led to his premature return from the Lions' tour occurred after 11 minutes of the match – and, for all that he had no idea at the time of the extent of the damage, he remembered it happening and knew perfectly well who did it.

It wasn't, he says, particularly painful on the field, rather 'a kind of drawing sensation…' Twice – once in the first half and again at half-time – he was medically examined by the tour manager, Dr Doug Smith, but not until the match was over and Carmichael was stretched out on a table in the dressing room with ice packs on his face, was it realised how badly he had been hurt.

In layman's language, the bones around the eye were broken in, as it were, three places out of four. One more break and he would have had to have the broken bones wired – though even that would not, one gathers, have precluded his playing again.

The greatest tragedy was that he had come by so serious a mishap when he not only appeared certain of his Test match berth, but also when he had been playing, by all accounts, probably the best rugby of a career that had already brought him 22 Scotland caps.
Norman Mair

New Zealand rugby will never be quite the same after the triumphant tour of John Dawes' Lions. In all aspects of this marvellous tour they set standards that further visiting sides will find difficult to match.

What team could so open the eyes of complacent New Zealanders to newer and brighter heavens of rugby in which the punt and the ruck are not the only gods?

True, the Lions' rampant progress must be measured against the fact that New Zealand rugby, through the loss of so many leading players in the last six months, is rather in a trough at the moment, and for sure the All Blacks never had a man of Carwyn James' acuteness to fashion their tactics.

But the 1971 Lions still became the first team since the 1937 Springboks to touch the fringe of greatness by winning all their non-Test games.

They have wakened New Zealanders, too, to the old-time artistry of threequarter play by Mike Gibson, Gerald Davies and David Duckham, and to the possibilities of counter-attacks such as those started by the gifted John Williams.
Donald Cameron

November 1971

Chris Wardlow, the big England centre, is not one to refuse a challenge. He made a big effort, en route to Japan with the England team, to master the use of chopsticks. 'It was all right till I came to the custard,' he said afterwards. Ah, well – at least he tried!

One of the sights of Scottish rugby last season was the spin pass of Edinburgh Wanderers' new scrum-half, Alan Lawson – a pass inspired less by the example of Chris Laidlaw and Gareth Edwards than by the requirements of Lawson's stand-off in his days at Strathclyde University, the talented, if perhaps rather lightly built, Douglas Arneil.

Alan Lawson readily admits that spin-passing rapidly became an obsession: 'I can think of four games at least I probably lost for Strathclyde by over-indulging in spin-

passing before I had sufficient mastery of the technique involved.'
Norman Mair

What price John Pullin as a possible captain of England? Hookers are not always favoured for this job, but Eric Evans, of Sale and Lancashire, made a big success of it in the 1950s.

Pullin, too, has garnered a lot of experience in 20 appearances for England and a couple of Lions tours. He is not one of the voluble types – front-row men rarely are – but Phil Judd, of Coventry, proved that this is not a 'must' for the job. Knowledge of the game, and how to react in an emergency, is what counts, and Pullin, by now, should be well endowed with this.
Vivian Jenkins

Every few years Scotland produces a great world-class player behind the scrum. Within my memory there have been Ian Smith – I refer to the Oxford University and Edinburgh University player of the 1920s – Arthur Smith, Ken Scotland and Gordon Waddell.

One who may well join this exalted band is Alastair Gourlay Biggar, whose rugby career has been extraordinarily successful since he left Sedbergh only six years ago. He is now 25, yet he has played against most of the great sides of the world.
Rupert Cherry

With three representatives – Dick Cowman, Chris Wardlow and David Robinson – in England's Far East squad and a fourth, Peter Dixon, having had such a successful tour with the Lions, Cumberland and Westmorland believe that this could be their year in the County Championship.

Not since 1924 have they won either the title or the northern group, but this season they have a special incentive, for it was in 1872 that the Two Counties Union was officially formed.

The one regret which county officials have is that Cowman, Wardlow, Robinson and Dixon all gained prominence through moving to other parts of the country. Cowman and Dixon both began their careers with Workington; Wardlow and Robinson with Carlisle.

December 1971

Quote by David Bain, president of the Bucks Referees Society and noted in that society's newsletter, after the Lions' defeat by Queensland on 12 May last:

'This Lions team will not be any good – too many b—— Welshmen. Let's face facts – Welshmen never play good rugby except for Wales!'

It looks as though we can expect a considerable extension of Sunday rugby in the next decade. Many clubs are fulfilling their new knock-out competition commitments in this way, and others are using it as a way of minimising the effect of Saturday televising of big matches on their club gates.

London Irish were pioneers in this direction. They played Rosslyn Park on a Sunday, and took £500 by way of programmes at 20p per time and car park fees. On a previous occasion, when one of their home fixtures clashed with a big match at Twickenham, the RU's centenary game, they played Bristol on the Saturday morning and the takings were only £22. So the Sunday trend looks like continuing.

Burly lock Alan Brinn recently played his 400th game for Gloucester. Also a regular choice in the Gloucestershire pack and a member of the England squad last season, Brinn's number of appearances for the cherry-and-whites is surpassed only by Peter Ford, now a regional selector, and Dick Smith and Mickie Booth, who are still playing for the club.

A World Cup Quiz

Compiled by Nigel Starmer-Smith

1. What was the score at full-time in the 1995 World Cup final between New Zealand and South Africa?

2. Two players between them scored all the points in the final. Who were they?

3. How many players took part in the final?

4. Who said: 'I took precautions. We drank the champagne before the match'?

5. Who were the four pool winners?

6. Which match of the World Cup finals produced the lowest total number of points?

7. Which match of the World Cup finals produced the highest total number of points?

8. Which countries failed to win a game in the World Cup finals?

9. Which two players scored the most tries (seven each) in the finals?

10. Who was the top points-scorer in the World Cup finals?

11. One player scored over 30 points in two separate games. Who was he?

12. How many tries were scored in the finals – was it 187, 207, or 147?

13. Who is the only player to have appeared in a World Cup final twice?

14. Who has scored the most tries in all World Cup final rounds?

15. Name the nine towns which hosted matches in the 1995 World Cup finals.

16. Who said to whom: 'You have done more for our country than we can ever do?'

(Answers on page 88)

Review of the
Season 1994-5

Save & Prosper have now been sponsoring English rugby for over a decade.

And, all in all, it's been a very successful period.

Just as it has for many of the thousands of people who have invested money with us through our unit trusts, PEPs and other savings and investment schemes.

If you'd like to know more about how we could help you get the most from your money, just call us on our free Moneyline 0800 282 101.

THE SAVE & PROSPER INTERNATIONALS

18 NOVEMBER 1995	ENGLAND v SOUTH AFRICA
16 DECEMBER 1995	ENGLAND v WESTERN SAMOA
3 FEBRUARY 1996	ENGLAND v WALES
16 MARCH 1996	ENGLAND v IRELAND

THE INVESTMENT HOUSE

UNIT TRUSTS • PEPS • PENSIONS • BANKING SERVICES

SAVE & PROSPER GROUP ONLY MARKETS ITS OWN PRODUCTS AND IS REGULATED BY THE PERSONAL
INVESTMENT AUTHORITY AND IMRO.

The Five Nations Championship

by Bill McLaren

If the number of tries scored decided the Five Nations Championship, France would have won four of the last five, the one exception being the 1992 tournament, when England achieved back-to-back Grand Slams by stitching together such admirable segments of the total game as to amass 15 tries in their four matches.

However, England have proved the dominant force in recent Championships and 1995 brought them not only their third Grand Slam in five years, but a haul of tries more in keeping with their Slam status than those of some previous seasons. Indeed, in the 1994 Championship England managed only two tries – by Rory Underwood and Tim Rodber against Wales. In the 1995 campaign, by contrast, they ran in nine and the only match in which they failed to score a try was Scotland at Twickenham, when Rob Andrew rose to the occasion with eight goals in victory by 24–12.

England demonstrated once again that they were a team for all seasons with that ability to fashion just the right tactical approach to suit the occasion and challenge. In their opening game against Ireland in Dublin, which they won 20–8, they held to a restricted style aimed at providing the Irish with as little loose fodder upon which to feast as possible. England opted to play against the tugging gale, a dangerous undertaking in Dublin, but their pack took such control of the ball and the action, with their big loose forwards, Tim Rodber, Dean Richards and Ben Clarke, in exceptional form, as to reach the interval 12–3 ahead and virtually home and dry.

In reaching a peak to defeat France 31–10 at Twickenham they moved the ball by hand more, forwards and backs combining with

Tony Underwood scores his second try of the match to polish off a magnificent team performance for England in their 31–10 victory over France at Twickenham.

"

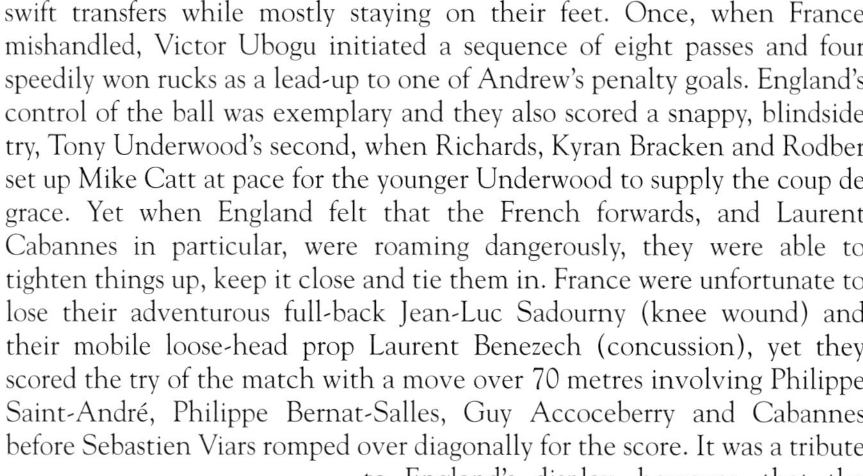

swift transfers while mostly staying on their feet. Once, when France mishandled, Victor Ubogu initiated a sequence of eight passes and four speedily won rucks as a lead-up to one of Andrew's penalty goals. England's control of the ball was exemplary and they also scored a snappy, blindside try, Tony Underwood's second, when Richards, Kyran Bracken and Rodber set up Mike Catt at pace for the younger Underwood to supply the coup de grace. Yet when England felt that the French forwards, and Laurent Cabannes in particular, were roaming dangerously, they were able to tighten things up, keep it close and tie them in. France were unfortunate to lose their adventurous full-back Jean-Luc Sadourny (knee wound) and their mobile loose-head prop Laurent Benezech (concussion), yet they scored the try of the match with a move over 70 metres involving Philippe Saint-André, Philippe Bernat-Salles, Guy Accoceberry and Cabannes before Sebastien Viars romped over diagonally for the score. It was a tribute to England's display, however, that the inimitable Philippe Sella rated them the best all-round England team he had played against with not a discernible weakness.

England's rumbling, rolling mauls were a key ingredient in their 23–9 defeat of Wales in Cardiff, in which Dean Richards became the most-capped No. 8 in the world, Ieuan Evans uncharacteristically mishandled a Robert Jones scoring pass at 10–3 and Neil Jenkins sent a drop-out straight at Ben Clarke for one of Rory Underwood's two tries. The outcome might have been a lot closer had Wales not lost Anthony Clement (concussion), Nigel Walker (dislocated shoulder) and John Davies (ordered off). As Wales did not have, on the field, a player equipped to take over the Davies role, flanker Hemi Taylor left the pitch to allow a regular prop, Huw Williams-Jones, to go on as a replacement.

The resurgence of the 1995 Five Nations was that of Scotland, who emerged from a run of nine games without a winning sequence to beat Canada (22–6), Ireland (26–13) France (23–21) and Wales

Rob Wainwright congratulates Eric Peters on what was arguably the best try of the Five Nations Championship, for Scotland against Wales at Murrayfield. Scotland ran out 26–13 winners.

(26–13). Contributing to this Scottish run was a selectorial gamble in the naming of three new forward caps, David Hilton (Bath), Stewart Campbell (Dundee HSFP) and Eric Peters (Bath). The selectors also omitted Scott Hastings and Doddie Weir, who were, however, restored later. Scotland had an important edge of pace from Gregor Townsend (Gala), as shown in his brilliant try against France in Paris, and there was a quite magnificent response to his critics by Gavin Hastings, who had a tremendous Championship, scoring a fairytale try in Paris and converting it to seal Scotland's first win there for 26 years. The reverse, inverted, one-handed feed with which Townsend launched Hastings on his historic scoring run will never be forgotten. A mighty performance by Damian Cronin in the line-out and elsewhere marked the 26–13 win over Ireland at Murrayfield in which Welshman Derek Bevan, refereeing his world-record 26th international, played advantage to perfection for Craig Joiner's try.

Following their Paris success, Scotland set up the Grand Slam decider against England with a 26–13 win at Murrayfield over Wales, who got off to a rocketing start, running in a try within two and a half minutes of the kick-off. It was to prove the only Welsh try of the Championship, and it was a beauty, scored by Robert Jones after a typical charge by Emyr Lewis. Scotland's loose forwards, however, made a big imprint on the action. One of them, Rob Wainwright, lit the touchpaper to arguably the try of the series. He fielded Wayne Proctor's punt and ran it back from deep. Gavin Hastings, Doddie Weir and Kenny Logan took it on and Eric Peters added the finishing touch.

The Slam decider proved something of a personal triumph for Rob Andrew. Not only did he score all of England's points, with seven penalty goals and one dropped goal (his 21st in an international), but his tally of 24 equalled the record for a Championship match, held by Sebastien Viars of France. Andrew also became England's highest scorer with 317 points, which he extended to 397 with his World Cup efforts. There were no tries: England were awarded 19 penalties to Scotland's nine and the nearest either side came to a try was when Gavin Hastings, who set a new Scottish record for a Championship with 56 points, had the ball knocked from his grasp by Mike Catt with Townsend in a scoring support position. Jason Leonard became England's most-capped prop and Scott Hastings Scotland's most-capped centre.

Wales had hinted at a revival in their spirited display against South Africa in which defeat by 20–12 masked their discovery of a line-out weapon in the person of the 6ft 10in Derwyn Jones (Cardiff), aided by the captain, Gareth Llewellyn (Neath). There was also some power running

Jeremy Guscott prepares himself for the crunch as Scotland captain Gavin Hastings closes in. This was one of the few attacking moments in an otherwise disappointing match.

from Mike Hall, who later captained Wales. The South African skipper, François Pienaar, reckoned the Welsh match was 'the toughest of our tour' and that Wales 'were much better than Scotland or Argentina'. Wales, however, did not carry such promise into the Five Nations Championship, in which, for only the second time, they finished with a whitewash, having suffered grievous defections and injuries and losing to France (9–21) in Paris, England (9–23) in Cardiff, Scotland (13–26) at Murrayfield and Ireland (12–16) in Cardiff. Wales have not beaten Ireland at home since 1983, and the latest Ireland win there featured a brilliant try by Brendan Mullin, an outstanding display by Welsh prop Spencer John of Llanelli and kamikaze tackling by the Irish. Wales were short of the launch-pads they needed for moving the ball by hand. There was also a wave of controversy over the omission of Derwyn Jones from the Irish match. There followed a change of national coach, Alex Evans, the Australian who had guided Cardiff to the League Championship, taking over from Alan Davies and Geoff Evans as manager from Robert Norster.

The French still hinted at their capacity for hitting on the break, as witnessed by the Viars try against England, but direction from their hinge was occasionally awry and it was only when they restored some of their veteran players against Ireland that they began to look the part again. Franck Mesnel (33), Marc Cecillon (35) and Louis Armary (31) all returned to the fray, which perhaps explained their turnover success against the Irish, who were still in the game at half-time, partly through the efforts in the line-outs of David Tweed (winning his first cap at the age of 35) and Gabriel Fulcher. France, with wind advantage, led only 3–0 at the interval but as their coach, Pierre Berbizier, said afterwards, 'We prefer to play with the ball in our hands, which is needed when you are against the wind.' In any event, France's Dad's Army proved more than adequate to the task, although it took a try by Yann Delaigue from the half-time kick-off, following beautiful linkage by Philippe Benetton, Accoceberry, Christian Califano and Philippe Saint-André, to convince them that they could win with a bit to spare.

The 1995 Championship spawned 31 tries, 11 more than in each of the previous two seasons, and, France apart, the differential between tries scored and tries conceded fairly reflected the Championship placings: England 9–2 (plus 7), Scotland 6–6 (nil), France 10–6 (plus 4), Ireland 5–9 (minus 4), Wales 1–8 (minus 7). It was therefore another part of England's armoury that they were defensively sound in conceding only two tries – to Anthony Foley (Ireland) and Sebastien Viars (France).

Sella was right. England had the power, the plan, the balance, the boot, the parsimony and the belief with barely a weakness. They deserved to be champions.

Ireland's Brendan Mullin celebrates his try against Wales. Ireland's 16–12 victory extended their unbeaten run at Cardiff – Wales have not defeated Ireland there since 1983.

The French pack surge towards the Ireland line during their 25–7 win at Lansdowne Road.

ANSWERS

to A World Cup Quiz (on page 80)

1. 9–9.
2. Andrew Mehrtens and Joel Stransky.
3. 37.
4. Pierre Berbizier, after France's semi-final defeat by South Africa.
5. South Africa, England, New Zealand, France.
6. The final. South Africa 15, New Zealand 12 (after extra time).
7. New Zealand v Japan, 145–17.
8. Romania, Argentina, Japan, Ivory Coast.
9. Marc Ellis and Jonah Lomu.
10. Thierry Lacroix, 112 points.
11. Gavin Hastings (44 v Ivory Coast; 31 v Tonga).
12. 187.
13. Sean Fitzpatrick (New Zealand).
14. Rory Underwood, 11 tries.
15. Johannesburg, Pretoria, Bloemfontein, Durban, East London, Port Elizabeth, Cape Town, Stellenbosch, Rustenburg.
16. François Pienaar, the Springbok captain, to President Nelson Mandela.

KEY PLAYERS FOR 1995-6

ENGLAND

MIKE CATT

KYRAN BRACKEN

Mike Catt is the most versatile back in English rugby. He has proved he is good enough to play international rugby at both fly-half and full-back and in fact first caught the eye of the rugby critics when he played a full season at centre for Bath. When Stuart Barnes retired in the summer of 1994, Catt switched from centre to fly-half, where he had already won one cap for England, coming on as a replacement for Rob Andrew against Wales in March 1994. His big break came when Paul Hull was injured in the match against Canada in December of that year and Catt replaced him at full-back. He had a magnificent match, and even though it was a very rare appearance for him in that position, and despite the fact that he continued to play at fly-half for Bath, he has become the established England full-back. He was a key figure in England's Grand Slam and went on to show several glimpses of his wonderful attacking running during their World Cup campaign. There has been a great deal of talk about England's new 15-man running approach to international rugby, but so far there has been precious little evidence of it. Mike Catt can change all that if he is given half a chance. He is quick, has a good eye for a gap and a neat side-step; he is a beautifully balanced runner and a natural footballer. He loves to attack, and if England do ever decide to employ his wide range of skills they could not only win another Grand Slam but do so with real style.

Just as the introduction of Mike Catt has added an extra dimension to England's back play, so too should the recall of Kyran Bracken at scrum-half. He has all basic skills of a classic scrum-half with the fastest service in English rugby. Instinctively, he has his feet in the correct position for every pass the moment the ball becomes available and he has remarkably quick hands in whipping the ball out to the fly-half. This speed and accuracy gives the whole back division more time and room to operate and should be the catalyst for a more expansive game. The most exciting back division in the 1995 World Cup was unquestionably that of the All Blacks, and it is certainly no coincidence that they had the brilliant Bachop at scrum-half. Kyran Bracken is in a very similar mould and he is fully capable of doing for the English backs what Bachop did for New Zealand. Bracken is a strong runner in attack and also a good defensive player. He is a useful kicker, too, and should be just the player to transform England's style of play. Dewi Morris was a tremendously committed scrum-half and it could be argued that he was just about the best England player in South Africa during the World Cup, but his strengths are quite different from those of Bracken. He has always been a more abrasive runner with the ball and a very physical player, both in attack and defence, but Bracken is definitely the man to breathe new life into the English back line.

FRANCE

EMILE NTAMACK

THIERRY LACROIX

A relative newcomer to the French team, Emile Ntamack made his international debut against Wales in 1994 and rapidly earned a reputation as a very fast, powerful wing. French rugby had suffered two disappointing seasons in the build-up to the World Cup and Ntamack did not have too many opportunities to show just what a strong and elusive runner he is. He has proved for his club side, Stade Toulousain, that he is an explosive runner of the highest quality and he emerged from the 1995 World Cup as one of the best wings in the world. He scored a superb match-winning try in the second minute of injury time against Scotland in the vital pool game which gave France a much easier route to the semi-finals. For that try, Ntamack sprinted 70 metres across the field from the right wing to take the ball inside the French left wing to score. Although he is not quite in the mould of the All Black left wing Jonah Lomu, it was generally agreed by the leading players and critics that Ntamack was the best right wing in the World Cup. With Philippe Saint-André on the other wing, France now have the best pair of wings in the northern hemisphere, and they also have a great running full-back in Jean-Luc Sadourny. If they can get the half-back selection right, they could well justify their position as the third-best side in the world.

The real problem for the French in the past four seasons has been to find a decent pair of half-backs and they do not look any nearer solving this. One possible solution would be to try Thierry Lacroix at fly-half, because he has almost all of the attributes which are important for that key position. He is an outstanding kicker with either foot and of course he just happens to be an excellent goal-kicker too. He has won countless games for France with his goal-kicking and he is about to overtake Didier Camberabero as the highest points-scorer in French international history. But he has now developed into something much more than that. He scored tries in the World Cup himself and made several others. He has become a strong midfield runner in attack and he is also an excellent support player – talents which would be very useful in a fly-half. Furthermore, he is an aggressive tackler in the centre and he could be extremely handy as a defensive player if chosen at fly-half because he would act as an extra flanker. It seems a terrible waste to have two magnificent wings and an exciting running full-back, as France have, as well as two positive attacking centres in Lacroix and the great Philippe Sella, only to find the half-backs guilty of wasting good possession over and over again. Playing Lacroix at fly-half could remedy one of the problem positions.

IRELAND

PADDY JOHNS

NEIL FRANCIS

The Irish have often produced tremendous loose forwards but in recent seasons, since the retirement of Donal Lenihan, they have struggled at the line-out. Now they have found a group of big forwards who can command respect as jumpers and, while they sort out the best and most promising of the younger generation, notably Foley, Corkery and Fulcher, they know that Neil Francis and Paddy Johns will guarantee a fair share of possession. It is possible now that Ireland will follow the example of South Africa, New Zealand, Australia and England and try to pack four genuine jumpers into their side – two at lock and two in the back row. If that is the case it could well be that Paddy Johns will play at No. 8. He certainly has the speed and the ball-playing skills for a No. 8, as he showed in his tremendous seven-a-side performances at the annual Cathay Pacific–Hongkong Bank Sevens. With the best players in the world taking part in Hong Kong every year, there can be no greater praise than to say that Paddy Johns is right up there with the best of them. A good jumper at the back, he is fast, creative and a very athletic forward. He was a key player in Ireland's World Cup campaign and he could well be a very influential forward this season, whether he plays at lock or at No. 8.

Life has been very difficult for Neil Francis in recent seasons in that he has been playing at lock forward for Ireland at a time when all too often he has been their only genuine top-class line-out forward. It is much easier for the opposition to destroy the chances of one outstanding jumper if they know the other seven forwards are not a real threat at the line-out. That has regularly been the fate of Francis, who finds he is the centre of the opposition's attention every time Ireland have the throw at the line-out. He has never enjoyed the luxury that, for example, Martin Johnson has with England. On an England throw, the opposition know that the ball could be thrown to Johnson or Bayfield or Richards or Rodber or Clarke. For the past four seasons, since the 1991 World Cup, Ireland's opponents have known that the ball will probably be thrown to Francis, which places an intolerable pressure on him. It now looks as if the Irish could well have three good jumpers, and that should be a huge help to Francis. He is a first-class line-out player and at his best he can take on any player in the world. His two-handed catching and accurate palming could be the launching-pad for a revitalised Irish pack to make their mark in the Five Nations after the disappointment of last season. Neil Francis could be their key forward, especially if they use a lot of short line-outs.

SCOTLAND

CRAIG CHALMERS

STEWART CAMPBELL

The most-capped fly-half in Scottish rugby, Craig Chalmers, should this season, barring injury, join that select band of players who have won 50 caps. He exploded on to the scene in 1989, when he rounded off a great first season in international rugby with a place on the British Lions tour to Australia. He played in the First Test on that tour and since then has been a key player for Scotland in the last two World Cups. A dropped-goal expert, he is a prodigious kicker of the ball as well as an aggressive tackler. A good passer, he has a very safe pair of hands and is a very good support player. He has a neat side-step and an eye for the gap and he has shown on many occasions that he can be a tricky runner. It says a great deal for him that he has remained a remarkably consistent player at the highest level with a variety of partners at scrum-half. Chalmers has been almost ever-present at fly-half while injuries have meant that he has played outside Gary Armstrong, Andy Nicol, Derrick Patterson and Bryan Redpath in the past three seasons. Scotland will surely miss Gavin Hastings this season, but the experience, talent and phenomenal competitive instinct of Craig Chalmers should ensure another very good year for the Scots.

The Scottish pack enjoyed a superb year in 1995 and a lot of credit should go to Stewart Campbell, who had an excellent first season of international rugby at the relatively young age for a lock forward of 22. At 6ft 6ins and nearly 17st he certainly looks the part, and after a brief apprenticeship with Scotland A against France, South Africa and Italy, he was chosen for Scotland's tour to Argentina. He had a successful tour and played particularly well for the Scotland Development XV against New Zealand in November 1993. He won his first full cap against Canada in January 1995 before going on to play in all the Five Nations matches. Scotland were the only one of the Four Home Unions to play to their full potential in South Africa at the World Cup, and Stewart Campbell gained further valuable experience and acquitted himself very well. He is a very good line-out jumper and a decent scrummager. For such a big player, he is very athletic and pretty lively in open play. He is now a crucial part of a mobile Scottish pack and his own game will benefit from having so many experienced established players around him in the back five. The Scots have not always found it it easy in recent years to win quality line-out possession, but Campbell will definitely give them real hope for the future. And the great thing is that he is much more than just a useful jumper.

WALES

GARETH LLEWELLYN

DERWYN JONES

The Welsh pack has been unconvincing for the past three seasons but at least in 1995 they discovered they had a real line-out presence with the lock-forward combination of Gareth Llewellyn at 6ft 6ins and Derwyn Jones at 6ft 10ins. The problem has been that they have lacked the right blend in their loose-forward combination to take advantage of their solid scrummaging and decent line-out possession, so the forwards have been outplayed in the loose far too often to build up any rhythm or confidence. Llewellyn is the sort of player to lead by example and bring out the best in the rest of the pack – he has been a good captain of his club side, Neath, and has also captained Wales. He led the national team in the summer of 1993 on their tour to Zimbabwe and Namibia as well as in internationals against France, Italy and South Africa. Although he was first capped in 1989 against New Zealand, he did not establish himself in the Welsh side until 1992. Still only 26 at the start of this season, he is now playing the best rugby of his career and not only does he look sure to reach 50 caps in the not-too-distant future, he could well go on to become the most-capped Welsh forward in history. He is an outstanding line-out jumper, a good scrummager and a lively performer in the open. If Wales build their pack round Gareth Llewellyn they should enjoy a much better season.

It seems that second-row forwards get bigger every year, and the latest recruit to the Goliath club of international locks is Derwyn Jones. He is 6ft 10ins and $18\frac{1}{2}$st and not surprisingly he made a substantial impact in his first season for Wales. He first came to prominence when he won Under-19 caps for Wales against Ireland and Scotland in the early 1990s and he went on to play for Wales A against Ireland A and France A. He made his full international debut against South Africa and although he was not fully established in the side for last year's Five Nations Championship, he looks sure to be a key player over the next few seasons. Only 25 years old, he is bound to improve as he gains experience, but he is already a formidable line-out jumper. With his tremendous height he has a massive advantage and he made some memorable two-handed catches last season. Considering his size, Jones is pretty athletic and mobile in the loose, but with the Welsh back row in disarray he did not have much opportunity to shine for Wales in the open. He would also have benefited from a great deal more variety in the line-out, but unfortunately Wales lacked much imagination in this area. With two good props to support them, Derwyn Jones and Gareth Llewellyn should win a lot of top-quality line-out possession, and if they get their loose-forward combination right, Wales definitely have the makings of a good pack.

THE CLUB SCENE

BATH'S APRIL BLUES
by Bill Mitchell

Left: Ben Clarke congratulates Tony Swift on scoring in his last match for Bath during their victorious Pilkington Cup final with Wasps. *Right*: Bath captain Jon Hall, who missed the match through injury, raises the Pilkington Cup.

It had to happen sooner or later, but the fact that Bath are no longer League champions owes as much to the excellence of Leicester as it does to the needs of various international managers, who denuded them of some of their top players when they were most needed. As a result they were well below strength in the run-in to the title – worse off than Leicester, who also had to make player sacrifices – and achieved something of a minor miracle in retaining the Pilkington Cup in style at Twickenham, when they were still unable to select the Scots David Hilton, Eric Peters and Andy Reed (who eventually missed World Cup selection because of injury) and the Ireland wing Simon Geoghegan.

To add to their problems, they found that Mike Catt and retiring skipper

Jon Hall had to miss the Cup final through injuries, though with a touch of panache they were able to leave hooker Graham Dawe and prop John Mallett (both England World Cup squad members) on the bench and still beat third-placed Wasps by a massive 36–16. So deposed League champions Bath may be, but they remain the team to beat and, if anything, their latest campaign earned them as much credit as did either of the seasons in which they achieved the double, since this time their success was gained in the face of adversity.

This is not to imply that Leicester, who were the first title-holders in 1987–8, were lucky champions: several points can be made to weaken such an argument, one of them being that the Tigers themselves contributed six players to the England World Cup squad and thus had to omit several of them at various times during the League's closing stages. Nevertheless, they virtually clinched the title with a 31–21 home win over the defending

The Leicester pack rumble towards the line during the Tigers' 31–21 success in the vital League match against Bath at Welford Road in April.

champions, with whom they had also crucially drawn at the Recreation Ground back in October. A fine mix of experience and youth, the East Midlanders have for several seasons been the kind of club which might punish any slips by others. All they needed to do was gain some more consistency, and once this was achieved they were set to win top honours.

The World Cup factor suggests that the Leagues are probably too large – at least for the top clubs, whose treasurers would doubtless be the most reluctant to see any reductions in competitive fixtures. By and large, Division 1 was more exciting than in recent seasons, the top prize being officially decided in Leicester's favour only on the final day. Wasps came an honourable third (which would have been better but for some unexpected defeats by 'weaker' opposition), and Sale celebrated their return to the top division by finishing fourth and finally ending Bath's unbeaten home League record, which stretched back to 1992.

To prove that past glories nowadays count for nothing, the final day of the campaign saw a situation where Harlequins had to win at Gloucester to survive if Northampton's trip to West Hartlepool, who had already just managed to escape, was successful. It was, but Quins, too, won to stay in the top competition and the unfortunate Saints went down instead. Their nerve-racking final moments were possibly attributable to the fact that their squad of star players did not always appear to be as committed to the cause as they should have been.

The three other Division 1 members – Orrell, Bristol and Gloucester – arrived at the last Saturday with their anxieties alleviated, but they and all the other teams in the competition will know that a few poor results can bring danger, and that is not a bad thing. They also are aware from Sale's success that promoted sides nowadays are not just there to make up the numbers; indeed, the only side moving up from the second flight for 1995 – Saracens – did so well that they could challenge for the big prizes if they manage to retain their best players.

Saracens were ahead in the table by such a large margin that the interest in Division 2 was confined to the relegation issue. As a sop to the top League clubs, only one team was to come down, and the New Year festivities had scarcely ended before Saracens were virtually back among the elite. At the foot of the table, meanwhile, as 29 April dawned, only Wakefield could feel certain of escaping the trapdoor and only Coventry had already disappeared down it. There were various hard-luck stories, but at the end of the day Fylde's narrow home defeat – ironically, by Wakefield – cost them their place and the two lowest sides made way for Bedford and Blackheath from Division 3. In that League a mostly unexciting campaign

Opposite page: The Harlequins front row of Mullins, Moore and Leonard prepare themselves for battle. Harlequins' poor record in 1994–5 meant that First Division safety was not guaranteed until the last match of the season.

ended with Clifton and Exeter becoming Division 4 sides in the new season, the former after only one campaign among better company.

The Division 4 competition was also settled early on with bookies taking no more bets, but it was nonetheless notable for yet another promotion coming the way of Rotherham, a lowly junior club in North-East 1 when the Leagues first started. Since then they have been quietly moving ever upwards and in No. 8 Richard Selkirk they had a player who had appeared in all their League matches until a brother's wedding in the Caribbean necessitated his absence on two Saturdays. Reading had not started in quite such humble circumstances, but the past season saw them ascend for a third consecutive time. The nearest challengers, Liverpool St Helens, were 11 points adrift of Rotherham and six behind Reading, while the luckless Askeans and Broughton Park dropped to the divisional fifth tournaments for 1995–6.

In fact, it was the latter divisions which brought the most thrills after the top flight. In 5 North, Walsall had to work hard to shake off the attentions of Kendal and Wade Dooley's Preston Grasshoppers, while all

Cambridge University's Richard Davies and James Reynolds celebrate the Light Blues' third try in the Varsity Match.

Bedford Queens enjoy their 11–10 victory against St Albans in the final of the Pilkington Shield.

Lydney had to do to take the top spot and promotion from 5 South was to win at Henley in their final match. But Henley failed to oblige; they beat Lydney by an astonishing 33–30 and the shadowing London Welsh's narrow win (19–13 at Metropolitan Police) saw them sneak through.

Relegation was a sad tale for Barker's Butts in 5 North as a late defeat at home to Wharfedale allowed Nuneaton to escape and left the Coventry team to join Hereford in junior rugby, but in 5 South there was seldom much doubt that Sudbury and Basingstoke would descend, and so they did.

Barker's Butts apart, the promoted teams from 1994–5 did well in higher company. Wharfedale consistently justified their place in the League and distinguished themselves along with Henley. Barking enjoyed a thoroughly satisfactory first term in senior company, and we now look with interest at Cheltenham (who were once a top club), Camberley, ambitious Worcester (Junior Club of the Year) and Sandal.

Other events during the season brought varying degrees of entertainment. Oxford and Cambridge atoned for last year's tedium with a thriller won deservedly by the Light Blues, while West London Institute (who will appear as Brunel University College next season) gained an extremely fortuitous victory in the BUSA (formerly UAU) final at Twickenham – 31–30 against Swansea. The Hospitals' Cup final was a dreadful display won by the better side, Charing Cross–Westminster, against St Mary's by two penalty goals to one. The game was no better than the uncouth behaviour of the rival supporters. It is not easy to think of any club that would want to welcome such a low-grade event in the future.

Twickenham was the scene for the Schools Day and three services matches, which were all most entertaining and produced surprising new champions in the Navy, who thrashed both the Army and Royal Air Force in turn to take the honours for the first time since 1988. Headquarters then presented another double bill as Bedford Queens won the Pilkington Shield in another exciting match against St Albans (11–10), before Bath's tour de force against Wasps in the Pilkington Cup. The superbly reconstructed ground then shut up shop with the Middlesex Sevens finals, which were well won by a John Liley-inspired Leicester, although the crowd's cheers had to be shared with Ithuba, a coloured team from South Africa on their first visit to Britain.

As we went to press changes were in the air which will leave us with a very different Rugby Union game in the future. Whether we like it or not, the game is professional, although the beneficiaries represent a small percentage of those who play. We have the simple choice of accepting the truth of this or losing our best players to some kind of circus, which might happen anyway. No one is too sure about how things will develop, but change is inevitable and the authorities must recognise this and make the best of the situation.

There are, however, still a vast majority of players who give no thought to cash rewards. Two such people were at the annual Flowers–*Rugby World* Awards lunch. One, the vast prop Simon Baker, runs a pub in Catford and will go anywhere at his own expense to get a game. The other, policeman and West Hartlepool lock John Dixon, has had to make huge sacrifices throughout his career to play for his club and retires with nothing but praise, especially for his wife and family and everyone else who has helped him to enjoy every minute of it.

Whatever the future holds, these two and many others like them are the real face of the game. Although it will undergo some unavoidable and dramatic changes over the next season, at the end of the day the same clubs who have swept the board recently will probably do so again.

THE YEAR OF UNCERTAINTY
by Sean Diffley

In China it's the Year of the Dog, or the cat, or pig, or something. In Ireland, as in all other Rugby Union countries, this is the Year of Uncertainty, of Great Indecision. The main difference is that the 1995–6 season began with a host of media stories of untold riches as a plethora of contracts were flourished, even as far as the denizens of the front rows.

That news from abroad stirred little action among the elite Irish players, however. So often nowadays, in international terms, the Irish tend to be a bit tardy, content to tag along in the wake of the action elsewhere. It is a fact that, for the third World Cup in succession, Ireland managed to qualify for the quarter-final stage in 1995. But even if that places the Irish in the top eight of world rugby, it does not automatically install them as a real power.

There is a fear in Irish rugby – that is, outside the 20 or 30 international squad members – that a real professional game would destroy the game in Ireland and render it a backwater, like the domestic soccer game on the island. Soccer provides the odd class player for teams abroad: think of Georgie Best, or Pat Jennings, or Roy Keane, who left the part-time Irish scene for the riches and fame of the game away from home. Irish rugby, too, could see the better players joining clubs in England, where the streets – or at least the leading club dressing rooms – might be paved with gold, and far, far more of it than would be available in Ireland.

As the changes in the game gathered momentum, the World Cup witnessed the swansong of team manager Noel Murphy, former coach, former selector, former Lion and Lions coach, who decided to retire from all rugby activity. The rather strange upshot was that the IRFU decided to take more time to think over appointing his successor, not to mention a coach and other selectors. As I said, the Year of Indecision – and in more ways than one. As his reign ended, Murphy was more and more convinced of the necessity of producing and concentrating on an elite squad for Ireland. While Murphy and the IRFU committee paid due deference to the role of the club, the basic unit of the game in Irish rugby, they also underlined the need for a change of emphasis if Ireland were to retain their position among the top rugby nations. The result was a restructuring of the fixtures for 1995–6. The Insurance Corporation All-Ireland League, which has proved such a success, will be run off in the early weeks of the season. This, as the IRFU announced, is 'to facilitate the inter-provincial games and the national side, which must remain our number one focus'.

Shannon's Billy O'Shea is poised to take on the Dungannon defence.

Four seasons ago, when the All-Ireland League was first introduced to provide the first real national club competition, the hope was that it would revolutionise the Irish game. But it is now clearly realised that, however competitive and vigorous the League may be, there is still too great a step up from club stuff to Test-match fare. Thus the emphasis is on the Inter-Provincial Championship and on making the leading players available for squad training more frequently and with less disruption to clubs.

The Munster success saga continued in the All-Ireland as Shannon became the fourth side from the province to win the First Division, following the victories in previous seasons by Cork Constitution and Shannon's Limerick neighbours, Garryowen and Young Munster. Shannon's most noteworthy achievement in taking the title was that they became the first club to complete their ten League ties undefeated. And Mick Galwey's men conceded only 60 points (scoring 162), which was a remarkable defensive record, much better than that of any side in any of the four divisions comprising 44 teams.

The Dublin side Blackrock College made a valiant effort to prise the title away from Munster, but despite some spectacular open rugby, they could finish only second. A consolation was that their ten-match programme produced 228 points, easily the highest total in all four divisions.

The Munster clubs in Cork, and especially in Limerick, have a special enthusiasm for the All-Ireland League with which the other provinces' clubs are only slowly coming to terms. And there are no signs that the League, or at least the First Division title, will be taken away from them in 1995–6. There has been remarkably little movement in terms of players changing clubs for this season, among the top players anyway. The only notable transfer was that of Ireland's successful openside flanker David Corkery, who has joined the Dublin Second Division side Terenure College from Cork Constitution.

A highly significant addition to the growing staff at IRFU headquarters was that of Ray Southam as director of rugby development. Southam, originally from Wales, had been in New Zealand for the previous 25 years, and was much involved in coaching there. Conscious of the ever-present problems in standards of refereeing and of the difficulties of persuading people to take up the chore, the IRFU have enlisted the help of international referee Owen Doyle, who has taken upon himself the onerous task of 'coaching' and encouraging referees on a national basis. Doyle, who has had a distinguished international career over the past 11 seasons, will hang up his whistle to concentrate on his new role.

Since Lansdowne Road is the oldest of the regular international Test-match grounds – the first international there was played in March 1878 – the IRFU are debating whether a change of site is now called for. There is little scope for expanding the ground in its crowded environment near the city centre, so a sub-committee of the IRFU is looking at alternative ideas. Already 100 acres have been purchased at a greenfield site to the south-west of the city. The sub-committee are also having discussions with a large international leisure development company which has ambitious plans for developing the now defunct Phoenix Park Racecourse, a site where there are plans to build a multi-purpose football stadium. Significantly, at the IRFU AGM in June 1995, the outgoing president, Ken Reid, said he felt that 'single-purpose football stadia are things of the past'.

The sub-committee of the union which is charged with investigating all the possibilities is to report to the IRFU later this year. With more than £16 million on deposit and the Lansdowne Road ground very conservatively valued at around £8 million, the IRFU obviously have the option of either building a new ground on the outskirts of the city or entering a mutually beneficial partnership.

The Shannon players celebrate their success in the All-Ireland League. They became the first side to win the title without losing a game.

DRAMATIC DEVELOPMENTS IN SCOTLAND
by **Norman Mair**

A peppery colonel in his army days, Alf Wilson, president of the SRU in 1972–3, was an unrepentant reactionary remembered, with good-humoured affection, on two counts in particular.

First, Alf, a Scottish international and manager of the 1959 Lions, was one SRU dignitary whom no one would ever have accused of being two-faced. It was always said of him that even granted the bottomless resources of the English language, it would have been impossible for him to have been ruder behind your back than he was to your face. Secondly, there was his immortal summation of the SRU's attitude to change over the first 100 years of their existence: 'We say no – then think about it.'

Actually, even in his day, the SRU had one moment which was positively avant garde, namely when they pioneered the short overseas tour, travelling to South Africa in 1960 with their opening match the only Test of the trip. Which was pretty bold considering that, at the previous time of asking, Scotland had lost at home to the Springboks by 44–0. Since, then the SRU have often been prepared to lead the way, even though their image of a body dragged grunting and grumbling into the 20th century has still clung to them. Until, that is, two days in the August of 1995.

On 7 August, they revealed that Jim Telfer was to become a salaried, track-suited chairman of selectors, combining the post with that of national coaching director and SRU director of rugby. Never mind the titular smokescreen; the press saw him as Scotland's first paid team manager and said so. What the Fourth Estate could not deny was that it made absolute sense. Telfer was clearly the best man for the job, and as for the workload, he had always thrived on being so stretched. In 1984, when he coached Scotland to their first Grand Slam in 59 years, he was a deputy headmaster in Livingston, 15 miles west of Edinburgh, and a hotelier in Selkirk, which is 40 miles south of the Scottish capital.

On 8 August, Freddie McLeod, one of Scotland's representatives on the council of the IB, outlined the SRU's submissions to the meeting, which lay hard ahead, of the IB in

Jim Telfer is to become the first salaried chairman of selectors.

Paris. To those who had not read the wind, the proposals were sensational. They still spoke of trust funds rather than of players being paid to play, though McLeod, with commendable frankness, acknowledged that it amounted to much the same thing. To his mind, the time had come when the very word 'amateur' should be expunged from the laws governing Rugby Union – a view which is hardly new but which, coming from within the SRU, was regarded by the outside world as roughly tantamount to a papal bull espousing polygamy.

As McLeod and the SRU's chief executive, Bill Hogg, the only other SRU official present, made their way from the President's Suite at Murrayfield after this momentous press conference, they had to pass the banked portrait gallery of past presidents. 'I wouldn't,' advised a veteran scribe, 'catch their eye if I were you!'

The SRU chief executive, Bill Hogg.

One way and another, those two days in August provided a dramatic and wholly unprecedented prelude to a season which had itself been totally restructured. What was more, even the main sponsors, though still brewers, were new – McEwan's, who had served Scottish club rugby nobly, having given way to Tennents. All four divisions of the new Premier League had been scheduled to finish by the end of November, but there would be regional leagues thereafter wherein, in the absence of luminaries by then concentrating on the major representative scene, young players would get their chance in club first XVs.

It had to be noted that the long-awaited Scottish Cup – to be known as the SRU Tennents 1556 Cup, in deference to the sponsors' long history as brewers – would not reach its climax until May, which was going to be less than ideal in terms of players badly in need of a break before Scotland's tour of New Zealand. In the SRU Tennents Championship, the Premier League would feature a Division 1 of just eight clubs but with home and away fixtures (the 14-club Division 1 it replaced had been single-fixture).

To understand the debate, you had to understand the history of the game in Scotland. For instance, Scotland won eight and drew one of their first ten matches with Wales. Assuredly, there was no suggestion then of the men of the Principality being intrinsically better rugby players. But because of the difference in the way the game evolved in the two countries, Wales long ago overhauled that early deficit and today, despite their recent vicissitudes, lead Scotland by 54 wins to 43, with two games having been drawn.

In Wales, Rugby Union was, as everyone knows, largely classless and developed round such open clubs as Cardiff, Newport and Swansea, to cite but three. In Scotland, other than in the relatively thinly populated Borders, it was much more middle class and mostly thirled to the old school tie. That, in turn, meant all too many closed clubs dependent on the former pupils of just one school, a structure which predictably looked more and more flawed as the 20th century unfolded.

Had rugby in Scotland been primarily based on city sides such as Edinburgh and Glasgow, it is not impossible that Edinburgh, Glasgow and the Scottish Borders would eventually have given Scotland a framework not all that dissimilar to Australia's New South Wales, Queensland and Australian Capital Territories.

The now-retired secretary of the Rugby Football Union, Dudley Wood, was quoted last season as saying that England had a little matter of 375,000 players; Scotland have a mere 25,000. Compounding Scotland's numerical disadvantage had always been the dilemma of too many clubs chasing too little talent. A Division 1 of just eight clubs could have as dramatic an effect on the game north of the border as did the coming of the National Leagues in 1973–4 – another development in which Scotland had left their rivals open-mouthed by showing the way. One by one the other Home Unions followed suit. The Leagues had sounded the death knell of the closed clubs, at least as far as the upper echelons were concerned. Indeed, the day arrived when Edinburgh Academicals met Boroughmuir in an important top-of-the-table clash at Raeburn Place with just one erstwhile

Scrum-half Bryan Redpath leaves the defence in his wake during Melrose's game against Gala.

Academy boy apiece – Ford Swanson for the Academicals, Barrie Brown for Boroughmuir.

Now, quite deliberately, there is to be a much tighter congregation in Scotland of the best players available. 'Too tight,' fears Scotland's director of rugby. Telfer is worried that some of the great clubs of the past, which have provided Scotland with some wonderful performers but which are probably always going to be too small to survive in the rarefied environment of an eight-club Division 1, will lose so many of their players that they will decline to the point where they are no longer the breeding-fields of yesteryear. Telfer warns that even Melrose, who were the McEwan's Scottish champions three times in four years in the early 1990s, could one day find themselves up against it simply because the town itself is so small.

What most alarms Telfer, however, is the possible rise of a 'super six', a class above the annual relegation battle. 'It would be worse still,' he argues, 'if too many of those clubs were based in Edinburgh, as could well be the case. Much, much better if Glasgow, Dundee and so forth have a presence in Division 1.'

All of which is why he would – controversially – much prefer to see the new set-up superseded in the near future by an 11-club single-fixture Division 1 on the lines of the All-Ireland League. The clubs would play five home matches and five away, leaving plenty of room for a lot more in the way of district rugby on the lines of the state and provincial rugby which is such a feature of the game in New Zealand, Australia and South Africa: the three countries which, entirely significantly, in Telfer's opinion, also happen to be the first three winners of the World Cup.

Stirling County's Kenny Harper is stopped in his tracks during his side's match against Watsonians.

HIGHER STANDARDS NEEDED IN RUGBY'S BRAVE NEW WORLD
by David Stewart

Any review of the Welsh club scene is set against the backdrop of a national side whitewashed in the Championship and home early from the Rugby World Cup in South Africa, where only the little Japanese were beaten. The season is reflected neatly in the experiences of a variety of coaches. Alan Davies and Gareth Jenkins, together with manager Bob Norster, walked the gangplank provided by the WRU. Their short-term replacements had respectively been in charge of the winners of the Heineken League and the SWALEC Cup and the runners-up in each. Alex Evans (Cardiff), Mike Ruddock (Swansea) and Dennis John (Pontypridd) all had cause for satisfaction in the achievements of their clubs.

Cardiff finally won the League at their fifth attempt. It was nothing less than the club's expectation in Evans' third year at the end of a period of heavy investment in playing, coaching, administration and ground facilities. They scored 81 League tries, comfortably the most, and recorded some huge wins, notably against their old rivals Pontypool, both home and away. In many ways their success encapsulated the main problem in Heineken Division 1, namely that there are too many uncompetitive matches. The strong clubs seem to be getting stronger and the weak going in the other direction, some possibly never to reappear.

The strong Cardiff squad, now led by New Zealander Hemi Taylor, will next seek a Cup and League double. Only time will tell whether the suspicion that they are not quite good enough is well founded. The return of Mike Rayer following a badly broken leg will help, as will the experience gained by Taylor, Stuart Roy, Derwyn Jones, Mark Bennett, Andy Moore, and new Wales skipper

Hemi Taylor acts as a scrum-half in Cardiff's top-of-the-table clash with Swansea. Taylor will lead Cardiff in the defence of their League title in the 1995–6 season.

Jonathan Humphreys as a result of their exposure to international rugby in the last 12 months.

Both Swansea and Pontypridd would argue Cardiff's claim to being the best overall team last year. Perhaps the All Whites have a little more justification. Their Cup win was popular and deserved and they continue to play an exciting brand of football. Their squad, a mix of promising youth and classy experience, looks good for the year ahead. In the former category come prop Chris Loader, wing Alan Harries, lock Andrew Moore and No.7 Rob Appleyard, and in the latter Aled Williams, Paul Arnold, Garin Jenkins (if not lost to English club rugby), Anthony Clement, and two particularly committed men of West Glamorgan in Stuart Davies and Robert Jones. The scrum-half has a genuine love of the place, and despite the attractions of Cape Town – where, sadly, he again suffered knee problems – has declared he will never leave.

Dennis John is another coach who will take comfort from the loyalty his players show their club. Despite international commitments, Neil Jenkins played most of Pontypridd's matches, and once again was top scorer in the Heineken League with 249 points. During the fifth season of the League, he became the first player to pass the 1,000-point barrier. He was well served by scrum-half Paul John, son of Dennis, who in turn was provided with a formidable platform in which locks Greg Prosser and Mark Rowley, and Kiwi No. 8 Dale McIntosh, stood out. Veteran prop Nigel Bezani continues as captain for his fourth season.

Can Pontypridd maintain their momentum and finally turn it into a trophy? Losing the League to Cardiff by two points and the Cup to Swansea 12–17 sums up how narrow is the gap they must seek to close. Pontypridd are now being challenged by near neighbours Treorchy. The quoted objective for the self-styled Rhondda Zebras

Neil Jenkins is challenged by Bridgend's Gareth Thomas during Pontypridd's 22–6 victory.

Spencer John –
one of a number
of promising
young players
emerging through
the Llanelli ranks.

was a top six finish in their first year in Division 1. They did better than that: they came third. Admittedly, they had the same number of points as Neath, one more than Bridgend and two more than Swansea, and a couple of the end-of-season fixtures were, shall we say, not as competitive as they might have been. Treorchy were the grateful beneficiaries. Their reward was a fixture against the touring Fijians. An improving and committed squad of players, under the coaching direction of Loughborough graduate Clive Jones, will have the respect of all clubs in the season ahead. Having come so far so quickly, their task now is to consolidate their position. The club is well organised off the pitch, with a sound commercial basis and a dedicated spectator following.

Neath had a slightly quiet year by their own very high standards. As usual they delivered some mighty performances, notably against the touring South Africans, although on that occasion the mixture was laced with an unwelcome element of misplaced aggression (to be blunt, the game could not be described as rugby – all-in wrestling would have been closer to the mark). There was a sense of something just missing at the Gnoll. It was fuelled by the departure of the respected David Pickering as coach. Skipper Gareth Llewellyn and world-class prop John Davies were unstinting over and above their efforts for Wales. One to watch is Chris Wyatt, a big, athletic back-row forward. If his temperament can be sorted out, he may well move up a level.

A player who has already achieved that is outstanding Bridgend centre Gareth Thomas, capped in both his favourite position and on the wing in the World Cup. The task of club chief executive Steve Fenwick now is to keep him out of the hands of Rugby League. Appointing Thomas as a club development officer is a good start. He has already been followed into the Welsh XV by co-centre Gareth Jones. How much longer before outstanding scrum-half and captain Rob Howley makes the same progress? Bridgend played some exciting football, though they were handicapped by a lack of bulk up front. Llanelli had a forgettable season. Gareth Jenkins will return to the club with which he has a strong mutual affection. Assisted by the likes of Rupert Moon, Nigel and Phil Davies, apparently no longer required at international level, and strong young players in Spencer John and Craig Quinnell, his drive should lead to a turn in fortunes.

It was an awful year for Gwent clubs. Newport, Newbridge, Abertillery and Pontypool filled four of the bottom five slots in Division 1. Canadian captain Gareth Rees played a part in keeping the Rodney Parade club above water before a sending-off at Swansea ended his interest in the season. Pontypool, with only four wins, were unable to repeat their Houdini act of 12 months earlier. Bobby Windsor had stood down as coach to be replaced by Graham Taylor of Hawke's Bay in a bold attempt to sort out matters quickly. The popular Dunvant club were one point shy of survival. However, they have a good coach in Brian Thomas and a sound squad of players, who, having come up through the club's youth ranks, should stay put.

Aberavon and Ebbw Vale were promoted from the Second Division from which Narbeth and famous Old Penarth were relegated to Division 3. Promoted from the Third Division were Swansea Valley club Ystradgynlais and Caerphilly, who have gone from the Fourth to the Second. Fourth Division champions were Cardiff Institute, formerly Cardiff College of Education, whose old boys include Lyn 'The Leap' Davies, Gareth Edwards, John Bevan and Allan Martin, whose son Steve was a regular supplier of line-out ball last season.

Standards, so the argument runs, are not consistently high enough. The top players, paid or not, need to be playing to a high level every week. For the talent available, 12 teams is too many for the First Division, resulting in mismatches. Yet the WRU annual general meeting debated, but – mercifully – rejected, a motion to increase its size. What next? An Anglo-Welsh league? A European league backed by substantial TV money? One school of thought, which apparently has the sympathy of WRU chairman Vernon Pugh, is that the best four or five clubs must grow stronger (and accordingly richer) to compete in whatever the brave new world brings, and, it is hoped, the attendant increase in skills and fitness would be transmitted to the national XV. Certainly something is needed to perk up interest in the old game because, just now, optimism is at a premium in the south Wales coalfields, a traditional heartland of the game.

THE BEGINNING OF A NEW AGE
by Chris Thau

The year 1995 was unusually eventful, even by French standards. The entire season was geared towards a climactic World Cup. The Five Nations – with Scotland breaking the jinx of Parc des Princes and recording their first ever win against France at the Paris ground – was mediocre, but it was viewed as a mere stage in the build-up to better things in South Africa. France finished a credible third in the World Cup after an act of escapism against Scotland and a dramatic clash with South Africa, in which 10cm robbed Saint-André and his companions of a place in the final. Yet the French team somehow failed to deliver the goods for which their passionate supporters had been waiting. However, in addition to the bronze medals which secured them a place among the last 20 in 1999, they managed to beat England, a feat that has eluded them since the 1980s.

In the aftermath of the tournament the Kerry Packer affair brought out the worst out of the greedy brigade. To his credit, Philippe Sella refused to sign up and tarnish his role-model status. Guy Laporte resigned as manager amid rumours of differences between him and coach Pierre Berbizier during the World Cup. French legend André Herrero was appointed manager, apparently without the knowledge of Berbizier, which stirred up a storm in a teacup.

In South Africa Toulouse fly-half Christophe Deylaud disappointed his crowds of admirers. He was consistently under par, but Berbizier, in a rather Messianic mood, decided not to replace him with Mesnel. Deylaud failed to recapture the royal form displayed in the French club final, in which his mesmerising melange of skill, control, subtlety and scoring power sunk Castres without a trace. With Deylaud in the driving seat, the Rolls-Royce of French rugby, Stade Toulousain, won the French championship for the 12th time in their history, leaving Béziers, with 11 championships, trailing in their wake. Toulouse were favourites to take the title after the providential Ntamack scored the winning try, with Toulouse trailing 9–10, in the dying seconds of their game against Bourgoin–Jallieu.

The losing finalists, Castres Olympique, somehow discounted as a serious contender, surprised the pundits when they reached the final for the second time in three

Christophe Deylaud shows his kicking skills for Toulouse. The fly-half disappointed many with his form in the World Cup.

years, suggesting that rugby in the city is in a very healthy state. A combination of shrewd management in the persons of president Jean-Pierre Revol and general manager Gerard Cholley of 1977 Grand Slam fame, and the technical expertise of technical director Jacques Chabrol and two unpretentious but capable coaches, Thierry Merlos and Jean-Marie Barsalou, has taken Castres within sight of the magic Bouelier de Brennus once again.

The Toulouse players celebrate their 31–16 victory over Castres, which brought them the French championship title for the 11th time in the club's history.

The ecstatic Toulouse captain Albert Cigagna, the son of an Italian immigrant who was convinced by his son's rugby prowess to accept his son's change of nationality at the age of 16, has established a record difficult to surpass; this was his fifth Bouelier (and his third as captain) in eight attempts. To set the seal on a superb career, up to that point devoid of international glamour except for a couple of minor A selections a few years ago, Cigagna became, at 35, the oldest player to win a French cap when he was flown in as a replacement for the injured Philippe Benetton in the World Cup.

His selection symbolises everything that is both wrong and sublime about French rugby. On the one hand Cigagna was never a member of the French squad, and as such he had not been involved in preparations for the World Cup. On the other, his majestic performance in the French Championship final must have convinced Pierre Berbizier to call him to the service of the Republic literally at the end of his playing career. As one French scribe rhetorically put it: 'If he was not good enough he should not have been selected. But if he was good enough to play for France in a World Cup game, then why wasn't he selected in the first place?'

At the other end of the scale, the dejected Toulouse hooker Patrick Soula, one of the local heroes, tested positive for a stimulant after the club final. An unlikely drug-user, Soula is obviously guilty of carelessly taking a medicine without medical advice. What a sad way to finish a superb playing career.

During the silly season, the French Fédération, after 49 years at 7 Cité d'Antin, near l'Opéra, moved its headquarters to the nearby Rue de Liege, right behind Gare St Lazare. It is a pragmatic act dictated by the needs of an ever-growing corporation as well as a symbol of the changing times. August 1995: the end of an era, the beginning of a new age.

The Cité d'Antin house, built in 1829–30, was bought in 1946 by the then FFR president, Alfre Eluere. It has been the centre of French rugby politics and intrigue ever since. It has seen the demise of Eluere, following the upheaval created by his decision to abolish the Championship at the request of the Four Home Unions. Former international centre René Crabos, the representative of provincial France, took over in 1952. He resided at Cité d'Antin until 1962, when he was replaced by Jean Delbert.

At the time, running the affairs of FFR was a delicate balancing act between the incumbent president and one Georges Pautot, who in 1917 became administrative secretary, a position held today by the very capable Jean-Louis Barthes. Pautot ran the Fédération and French rugby in conjunction with his associate Madame Annette, who was in charge of the FFR personnel. Such was their power that it is said that they had even interfered in the selection of the French team. One day Lucien Mias, irritated by the continual meddling, told Madame Annette: 'Lady, you look after the administration, I am in charge of the French team.'

French rugby is notoriously unruly and prone to upheavals. Under Ferrasse it prospered and the FFR became one of the most respected unions in the world. Cité d'Antin became the symbol of the newly found French confidence. For more than 20 years Ferrasse dealt with dissent decisively, occasionally ruthlessly. He ran French rugby unchallenged until his coalition of old-time friends and associates known as 'Les Barons' collapsed within a short period of time. The painful public split with Guy Basquet left him isolated, and therefore vulnerable at the top.

Bernard Lapasset, who became president of the FFR in December.

The then heir apparent, Jacques Fouroux, launched his coup as soon as Basquet appeared to have been sidelined. Fouroux won the battle in the Cité d'Antin house in November 1990, but lost the war when the wounded lion, Ferrasse, struck back with a vengeance a few months later. In December 1991, the youthful former president of the Ile de France *département* and FFR secretary Bernard Lapasset became the new FFR president. In a way, the election of Lapasset, a senior customs and excise official in Paris, brought the cycle to an end. After 39 years, the Parisians had recaptured the FFR presidential office.

The Whitbread Flowers/*Rugby World* Awards 1995

(1) Player of the Year	Gavin Hastings
(2) International Player of the Year	François Pienaar
(3) Senior Team of the Year	Cardiff
(4) Most Promising Player	Mike Catt
(5) Junior Club of the Year	Worcester
(6) The Photograph of the Year	Russell Cheyne
(7) For Services to Journalism	Terry Cooper
(8) Coach of the Year	Jack Rowell
(9) Referee of the Year	Derek Bevan

A Summary of the Season

compiled by BILL MITCHELL

INTERNATIONAL RUGBY

Argentina in South Africa

September–October 1994

Opponents	Results	
SA Development XV	W	50 – 21
Border	W	41 – 25
South Africa A	L	12 – 56
SOUTH AFRICA	L	22 – 42
North Orange Free State	W	64 – 27
SOUTH AFRICA	L	26 – 46

Played 6 Won 3 Lost 3

South Africa
in Wales, Scotland & Ireland

October–December 1994

Opponents	Results	
Cardiff	W	11 – 6
Wales A	W	25 – 13
Llanelli	W	30 – 12
Neath	W	16 – 13
Swansea	W	78 – 7
Scotland A	L	15 – 17
Scottish Districts XV	W	33–16
Scottish Selection	W	35 – 10
SCOTLAND	W	34 – 10
Pontypridd	W	9 – 3
WALES	W	20 – 12

Combined Irish Provinces	W	54 – 19
Barbarians	L	15 – 23

Played 13 Won 11 Lost 2

United States in Ireland

November 1994

Opponents	Results	
Irish Development XV	W	20 – 13
IRELAND	W	15 – 26
Irish Universities	L	9 – 11
Leinster	L	6 – 9

Played 4 Won 1 Lost 3

Romania in England

November 1994

Opponents	Results	
Oxford University	L	16 – 26
Cambridge University	W	27 – 18
ENGLAND	L	3 – 54

Played 3 Won 1 Lost 2

Canada in Europe
November–December 1994

Opponents		Results
Italy B	L	11 – 18
Combined Services	L	20 – 21
England Emerging Players	L	6 – 34
ENGLAND	L	19 – 60
French Selection	L	21 – 24
FRANCE	L	9 – 28

Played 13 Won 12 Lost 1

Western Samoa in South Africa
April 1995

Opponents		Results
Northern Transvaal	L	13 – 23
Natal	L	17 – 21
SOUTH AFRICA	L	8 – 60
Transvaal	W	13 – 12
Northern Transvaal	L	16 – 52

Played 5 Won 1 Lost 4

Argentina in Australia
April – May 1995

Opponents		Results
ACT	L	16 – 33
AUSTRALIA	L	7 – 53
New South Wales B	L	16 – 42
AUSTRALIA	L	13–30

Played 4 Lost 4

Scotland in Spain
May 1995

Opponents		Results
Madrid XV	W	27 – 16
SPAIN	W	62 – 7

Played 2 Won 2

England A in Australia & Fiji
May–June 1995

Opponents		Results
South Australia	W	66 – 9
Victoria	W	76 – 19
Queensland XV	L	15 – 20
Australian Universities	L	30 – 32
NSW Country	L	23 – 28
Australian XV	W	27 – 19
FIJI	L	25 – 59

Played 7 Won 3 Lost 4

SCOTLAND A IN ZIMBABWE
JUNE 1995

Opponents	Results		
Mashonaland County	W	42 – 13	
ZIMBABWE	W	39 – 23	
Zimbabwe A	W	41 – 13	
ZIMBABWE	W	42 – 23	

Played 4 Won 4

THE BLEDISLOE CUP
JULY 1995

Australia	16	New Zealand	28
New Zealand	34	Australia	23

BARBARIAN FC
1994–5

Opponents	Results		
Bath	L	18 – 23	
French Barbarians	L	18 – 35	
Newport	W	54 – 45	
Swansea	L	17 – 39	
SOUTH AFRICA	W	23 – 15	
Leicester	L	18 – 31	
East Midlands	W	56 – 19	
Cardiff	L	33 – 75	

Played 8 Won 3 Lost 5

SUPER-10 TOURNAMENT
MAY 1995

POOL A

	P	W	L	D	F	A	Pts
Transvaal	4	3	0	1	78	65	13
NSW	4	2	1	1	78	64	11
W Province	4	2	0	2	99	106	9
Otago	4	2	0	2	102	91	8
N. Harbour	4	0	1	3	70	164	4

POOL B

	P	W	L	D	F	A	Pts
Queensland	4	4	0	0	116	48	16
OFS	4	3	0	1	85	81	12
Auckland	4	2	2	0	94	99	9
Canterbury	4	1	3	0	138	98	7
Tonga	4	0	4	0	62	159	1

Final
Transvaal	16	Queensland	30

CATHAY PACIFIC-HONGKONG BANK SEVENS
1995

Cup Final
New Zealand	35	Fiji	17

Plate Final
Canada	35	Argentina	12

Bowl Final
Hong Kong	45	Papua NG	7

The Five Nations Championship 1995

Results

France	21	Wales	9
Ireland	8	England	20
England	31	France	10
Scotland	26	Ireland	13
France	21	Scotland	23
Wales	9	England	23
Ireland	7	France	25
Scotland	26	Wales	13
England	24	Scotland	12
Wales	12	Ireland	16

	P	W	D	L	F	A	Pts
England	4	4	0	0	98	39	8
Scotland	4	3	0	1	87	71	6
France	4	2	0	2	77	70	4
Ireland	4	1	0	3	43	86	2
Wales	4	0	0	4	43	86	0

Women's Rugby 1994–5

Results

England	25	Wales	0
Scotland	20	Ireland	3
Wales	25	Ireland	0
Scotland A	0	Italy	49
Scotland	10	Italy	12

Other International Matches 1994–5

Results

Ireland U21	12	England U21	8
Wales U21	20	Romania U21	8
Scotland A	18	Italy A	16
Ireland A	20	England A	21
Scotland A	9	France A	13
Scotland	22	Canada	6
France A	15	Wales A	21
Scotland U21	22	Ireland U21	24
Scotland A	24	Ireland A	18
England A	29	France A	9
France U21	35	Scotland U21	12
Japan	25	Tonga	6
Scotland U21	15	Wales U21	9
Wales U21	16	Ireland U21	9
Wales A	30	Ireland A	19
Natal	33	England A	25
Romania	15	France	24
Fiji	15	Canada	24
Scotland U21	36	Italy U21	15
Scotland	49	Romania	16
Japan A	25	Romania	30
Japan	34	Romania	21
Italy	22	Ireland	12
Italy U21	6	England U21	22

World Youth Championship Final

France	27	Argentina	12

RUGBY WORLD CUP 1995

POOL A

South Africa	27	Australia	18
Canada	34	Romania	3
South Africa	21	Romania	8
Australia	27	Canada	11
Australia	42	Romania	3
South Africa	20	Canada	0

POOL C

Japan	10	Wales	57
Ireland	19	New Zealand	43
Ireland	50	Japan	28
New Zealand	34	Wales	9
Japan	17	New Zealand	145
Ireland	24	Wales	23

POOL B

Italy	18	Western Samoa	42
Argentina	18	England	24
Argentina	26	Western Samoa	32
England	27	Italy	20
Argentina	25	Italy	31
England	44	Western Samoa	22

POOL D

Scotland	89	Ivory Coast	0
France	38	Tonga	10
France	54	Ivory Coast	18
Scotland	41	Tonga	5
Ivory Coast	11	Tonga	29
France	22	Scotland	19

QUARTER-FINALS

France	36	Ireland	12	Australia	22	England	25
South Africa	42	Western Samoa	14	New Zealand	48	Scotland	30

SEMI-FINALS

South Africa	19	France	15	England	29	New Zealand	45

3RD–4TH-PLACE PLAY-OFF

France	19	England	9

FINAL

South Africa	15	New Zealand	12

CLUB, COUNTY AND DIVISIONAL RUGBY

ENGLAND

Pilkington Cup
Quarter-finals

Bath	26	Northampton	6
Exeter	0	Wasps	31
Harlequins	13	Wakefield	8
Sale	12	Leicester	14

Semi-finals

Harlequins	13	Bath	31
Leicester	22	Wasps	25

Final

Bath	36	Wasps	16

Pilkington Shield Final

Bedford Queens	11	St Albans	10

Courage Leagues
Division 1

	P	W	D	L	F	A	Pts
Leicester	18	15	1	2	400	239	31
Bath	18	12	3	3	373	245	27
Wasps	18	13	0	5	469	313	26
Sale	18	7	2	9	327	343	16
Orrell	18	6	3	9	256	325	15
Bristol	18	7	0	11	301	353	14
Gloucester	18	6	1	11	269	336	13
Harlequins	18	6	1	11	275	348	13
West H'pool	18	6	1	11	312	412	13
Northampton	18	6	0	12	267	335	12

Division 2

	P	W	D	L	F	A	Pts
Saracens	18	15	1	2	389	213	31
Wakefield	18	12	1	5	373	281	25
N. Gosforth	18	8	2	8	373	281	18
L. Scottish	18	9	0	9	351	221	18
London Irish	18	9	0	9	363	381	18
Moseley	18	8	1	9	299	303	17
Nottingham	18	8	1	9	299	322	17
Waterloo	18	8	0	10	287	331	16
Fylde	18	8	0	10	250	329	16
Coventry	18	2	0	16	213	436	4

Division 3 champions: Bedford
Runners-up: Blackheath
Division 4: Rotherham

Division 5 North: Walsall
Division 5 South: London Welsh

CIS County Championship
Semi-finals

Northumberland	14	Gloucestershire	13
Warwickshire	31	Berkshire	5

Final

Northumberland	9	Warwickshire	15

CIS Divisional Championship

	P	W	D	L	F	A	Pts
Midlands	3	3	0	0	72	48	6
London	3	2	0	1	76	51	4
North	3	1	0	2	59	76	2
South & SW	3	0	0	3	67	99	0

University Match

Oxford U.	21	Cambridge U.	26

University Second Teams Match

Oxford U.	11	Cambridge U.	19

University Under-21 Match

Oxford U.	19	Cambridge U.	21

British Universities Cup Final

Swansea	30	West London	31

Hospitals' Cup

Charing X-Westminster	6	St Mary's	3

Inter-Services Champions: Royal Navy
Securicor Trophy: British Police
Middlesex Sevens Champions: Leicester
Shell UK Ltd Rosslyn
Park Schools Sevens: Dwr-y-Felin
Open Winners: St Cyre's

WALES

SWALEC Welsh Challenge Cup
Quarter-finals

Cardiff	72	Aberavon	3
Llanelli	18	Bridgend	11
Newbridge	11	Swansea	19
Pontypridd	76	Mountain Ash	3

Semi-finals

| Cardiff | 9 | Swansea | 16 |
| Llanelli | 14 | Pontypridd | 20 |

Final

| Pontypridd | 12 | Swansea | 17 |

Heineken Leagues
Division 1

	P	W	D	L	F	A	Pts
Cardiff	22	18	0	4	672	269	36
Pontypridd	22	17	0	5	555	255	34
Treorchy	22	13	0	9	479	312	26
Neath	22	12	2	8	379	398	26
Bridgend	22	12	1	9	518	451	25
Swansea	22	12	0	10	475	400	24
Llanelli	22	10	0	12	459	409	18
Newport	22	9	0	13	366	433	18
Newbridge	22	8	0	14	302	452	16
Abertillery	22	8	0	14	349	604	16
Dunvant	22	7	1	14	333	542	15
Pontypool	22	4	0	18	293	655	8

Division 2

	P	W	D	L	F	A	Pts
Aberavon	22	17	0	5	506	263	34
Ebbw Vale	22	16	1	5	447	283	33
Abercynon	22	16	1	5	380	260	33
S. Wales Pol	22	12	2	8	413	357	26
Bonymaen	22	11	1	10	370	312	23
Maesteg	22	10	1	11	365	388	21
Tenby Utd	22	10	0	12	290	374	20
Llandovery	22	9	0	13	313	363	18
Llanharan	22	9	0	13	316	319	18
Cross Keys	22	8	0	14	292	438	16
Narberth	22	6	2	14	299	446	16
Penarth	22	4	0	18	289	477	8

Division 3 champions: Ystradgynlais
Runners-up: Caerphilly
Division 4 champions: Cardiff Institute
Runners-up: Pyle

SCOTLAND

McEwan's Inter-District Championship

	P	W	D	L	F	A	Pts
Exiles	4	4	0	0	119	51	8
Edinburgh	4	1	2	1	62	62	4
Nth & Mid.	4	1	1	2	69	84	3
S. of Scotland	4	1	1	2	61	81	3
Glasgow	4	1	0	3	62	95	2

Alloa Brewery Cup Final

| Boroughmuir | 42 | Dundee HSFP | 18 |

Castlemaine XXXX Trophy Final

| Forester FP | 22 | Garnock | 6 |

McEwan's National Leagues
Division 1

	P	W	D	L	F	A	Pts
Stirling Co.	13	11	1	1	234	162	23
Watsonians	13	9	0	4	298	212	18
Edinb'gh Ac.	13	7	2	4	216	141	16
Hawick	13	7	2	4	215	199	16
Heriot's FP	13	7	1	5	299	197	15
Boroughmuir	13	7	1	5	325	226	15
Gala	13	7	1	5	226	245	15
Melrose	13	7	0	6	308	261	14
G'gow H/K	13	6	1	6	228	183	13
Jed-Forest	13	6	0	7	221	256	12
W. of Scotland	13	5	0	8	166	233	10
Dundee HSFP	13	3	1	9	200	266	7
Currie	13	3	0	10	186	280	6
Stewart's/M.	13	1	0	12	158	321	2

Division 2

	P	W	D	L	F	A	Pts
Kelso	13	11	0	2	318	159	22
Selkirk	12	10	2	1	338	184	22
Kirkcaldy	13	8	1	4	271	230	17
Biggar	13	7	2	4	180	173	16
Preston L. FP	13	7	1	5	269	211	15
Glasgow Ac.	13	7	0	6	299	239	14
Peebles	13	7	0	6	175	204	14
Mussleburgh	13	6	1	6	253	223	13
Grangemouth	13	6	0	7	223	246	12
Corstorphine	13	5	1	7	180	214	11
Edinburgh W.	13	5	0	8	208	261	10
Wigtownshire	13	3	0	10	173	267	6
Gordonians	13	3	0	10	145	300	6
Haddington	13	2	0	11	178	275	4

Division 3 champions: Ayr
Runners-up: Kilmarnock
Division 4 champions: Glenrothes
Runners-up: Duns

IRELAND

Insurance Corporation All-Ireland Leagues

Division 1

	P	W	D	L	F	A	Pts
Shannon	10	10	0	0	162	160	20
Blackrock	10	7	0	3	228	135	14
St Mary's	10	7	0	3	151	137	14
Garryowen	10	6	0	4	160	113	12
Cork Const.	10	6	0	4	148	129	12
Old Wesley	10	5	0	5	131	171	10
Lansdowne	10	3	1	6	150	225	7
Instonians	10	3	0	7	111	160	6
Y. Munster	10	3	0	7	115	153	6
Sunday's W.	10	2	1	7	119	165	5
Dungannon	10	2	0	8	114	141	4

Division 2

	P	W	D	L	F	A	Pts
Old B'vedere	10	8	0	2	149	120	16
Ballymena	10	7	1	2	191	122	15
Wanderers	10	6	1	3	151	133	13
Terenure	10	6	0	4	187	171	12
Malone	10	5	0	5	143	139	10
Old Crescent	10	4	1	5	179	173	9
Greystones	10	4	1	5	173	194	9
Bective R.	8	4	0	4	126	93	8
Univ. Coll.	10	2	2	6	141	157	6
Dolphin	9	3	0	6	85	127	6
Bangor	9	1	0	8	83	161	2

Inter-Provincial Championship

	P	W	D	L	F	A	Pts
Munster	4	4	0	0	159	58	8
Ulster	4	2	0	2	84	51	4
Leinster	4	2	0	2	65	80	4
Exiles	4	1	0	3	77	117	2
Connacht	4	1	0	3	55	134	2

Senior Provincial Cup Finals

Leinster:

St Mary's College	29	Greystones	3

Munster:

Garryowen	23	Young Munster	3

Ulster:

Dungannon	21	Instonians	16

Connacht:

Buccaneers	14	Galwegians	12

FRANCE

French Club Championship

Semi-finals

Toulouse	16	Bourgoin	10
Castres	18	Toulon	13

Final

Toulouse	31	Castres	16

AUSTRALIA

Sydney Grand Final

Randwick	36	Warringah	16

NEW ZEALAND

Championship First Division

Semi-finals

Auckland	33	Otago	16
North Harbour	59	Canterbury	27

Final

Auckland	22	North Harbour	16

Ranfurly Shield Holders: Canterbury

SOUTH AFRICA

Currie Cup Final

Transvaal	56	OFS	33

FIXTURES

1995-6

AUGUST 1995

Sat 19	Kelso Sevens
Sat 26	Selkirk Sevens
Sun 27	South African Barbarians v Wales

SEPTEMBER 1995

Sat 2   SOUTH AFRICA v WALES
Tennents Premier Leagues 1 to 4
Tennents 1556 Cup
Heineken Leagues 1 to 5

Sat 9   Courage Leagues 1 to 4
Pilkington Cup 1st Round
Pilkington Shield 1st Round
Tennents Premier Leagues 1 to 4
Tennents 1556 Cup
Heineken Leagues 1 to 5

Wed 13   Tennents Leagues 1 to 4

Sat 16   Courage Leagues 1 to 4
Courage Leagues Other Divs
Tennents Premier Leagues 1 to 4
Tennents National Leagues 1 to 7
Heineken Leagues 1 to 5
Insurance Corporation Leagues 1 to 4

Sat 23   Courage Leagues 1 to 4
Courage Leagues Other Divs
Tennents Premier Leagues 1 to 4
Tennents National Leagues 1 to 7
Heineken Leagues 1 to 5
SWALEC Cup 1st Round
Insurance Corporation Leagues 1 to 4

Sat 30   Courage Leagues 1 to 4
Courage Leagues Other Divs
Tennents Premier Leagues 1 to 4
Tennents National Leagues 1 to 7
Heineken Leagues 1 to 5
Insurance Corporation Leagues 1 to 4

OCTOBER 1995

Tue 3   Newport v Barbarians
Sat 7   Courage Leagues 1 & 2

Pilkington Cup 2nd Round
Pilkington Shield 2nd Round
Tennents Leagues 1 to 4
Tennents National Leagues 1 to 7
Heineken Leagues 1 to 5
Insurance Corporation Leagues 1 to 4

Sat 14   Courage Leagues 1 & 2
Courage Leagues 3 & 4
Courage Leagues Other Divs
Tennents Leagues 1 to 4
Tennents National Leagues 1 to 7
Heineken Leagues 2 to 5
Insurance Corporation Leagues 1 to 4

Sun 15   Insurance Corporation Leagues Div 1:
Old Wesley v Lansdowne

Sat 21   Wales A v Fiji
Courage Leagues 1 & 2
Courage Leagues 3 & 4
Courage Leagues Other Divs
Tennents Leagues 1 to 4
Tennents National Leagues 1 to 7
Heineken Leagues 1
Heineken Leagues 3 & 4
SWALEC Cup 2nd Round
Insurance Corporation Leagues 1 to 4

Wed 25   Neath v Fiji

Sat 28   Cardiff v Fiji
Courage Leagues 1 & 2
Courage Leagues 3 & 4
Courage Leagues Other Divs
Tennents Leagues 1 to 4
Tennents National Leagues 1 to 7
Heineken Leagues 1, 2 & 5
Heineken Leagues 3 & 4

Mon 30   Combined Scottish Districts Under-21
v New Zealand *Rugby News* Under-21

NOVEMBER 1995

Wed 1   Treorchy v Fiji
Scotland U-21 v NZ *Rugby News* U-21

Sat 4   Pontypridd v Fiji
          Courage Leagues 1 & 2
          Pilkington Cup 3rd Round
          Pilkington Shield 3rd Round
          Tennents Leagues 1 to 4
          Tennents National Leagues 1 to 7
          Heineken Leagues 1, 2 & 5
          Heineken Leagues 3 & 4
Tue 7   Llanelli v Fiji
Wed 8   Edinburgh v Western Samoa
Sat 11   WALES v FIJI
          Courage Leagues 1 & 2
          Courage Leagues 3 & 4
          Courage Leagues Other Divs
          Tennents Leagues 1 to 4
          Tennents National Leagues 1 to 7
Sun 12   Scotland A v Western Samoa
Mon 13   Glasgow v Western Province
Tue 14   North & Midlands v Western Samoa
          Connacht v Fiji
Fri 17   South of Scotland v Western Province
Sat 18   ENGLAND v SOUTH AFRICA
          SCOTLAND v WESTERN SAMOA
          IRELAND v FIJI
          CIS Divisional Match :
              Midlands v London
          CIS County Championship Matches
          Heineken Leagues 1 & 2
          SWALEC Cup 3rd Round
Sun 19   CIS Divisional Match:
              South-West v North
          Tennents Leagues 1 to 4
          Tennents 1556 Cup 3rd Round
Tue 21   Oxford University v Western Samoa
Sat 25   CIS Divisional Matches :
              North v London
              South-West v Midlands
          CIS County Championship Matches
          Cambridge U v Western Samoa
          Tennents Premier Leagues 1 to 4
          Tennents National Leagues 1 to 7
          Heineken Leagues 1 to 4
          Heineken Leagues 5
          Irish Inter-provincial Matches:
              Exiles v Connacht
              Ulster v Munster
Wed 29   London Division v Western Samoa

DECEMBER 1995

Sat 2   Midlands Division v Western Samoa
          CIS Divisional Match :
              London v South-West
          CIS County Championship Matches
          Pilkington Shield 4th Round
          Tennents National Leagues 1 to 7
          Heineken Leagues 1 to 5
          Irish Inter-provincial Matches:
              Connacht v Ulster
              Exiles v Leinster
Sun 3   Scottish Exiles v South of Scotland
Tue 5   Northern Division v Western Samoa
Wed 6   Scottish Exiles v Edinburgh
          North & Midlands v Glasgow
Sat 9   South-West Division v Western Samoa
          CIS Divisional Match :
              Midlands v North
          CIS County Championship Matches
          Tennents Regional Leagues
          Tennents National Leagues 1 to 7
          Heineken Leagues 1 to 5
          Irish Inter-provincial Matches:
              Leinster v Connacht
              Munster v Exiles
Sun 10   Glasgow v Scottish Exiles
          South of Scotland v North & Midlands
Tue 12   Oxford v Cambridge
          Oxford Under-21 v Cambridge Under-21
          England A v Western Samoa
Sat 16   ENGLAND v WESTERN SAMOA
          Sun Alliance Colts County Championship
          CIS Divisional Championship Matches
          CIS County Championship Matches
          Tennents Regional Leagues
          Tennents National Leagues 1 to 7
          SWALEC Cup 4th Round
          Irish Inter-provincial Matches:
              Munster v Leinster
              Ulster v Exiles
Sun 17   North & Midlands v Scottish Exiles
          Edinburgh v South of Scotland
Fri 22   Scotland Schools v France Schools
Sat 23   Pilkington Cup 4th Round
          Pilkington Shield 5th Round
          Tennents Regional Leagues
          Heineken Leagues 1 & 2

Irish Inter-provincial Matches:
  Connacht v Munster
  Leinster v Ulster
Sun 24 South of Scotland v Glasgow
  Edinburgh v North & Midlands
Wed 27 Leicester v Barbarians
Sat 30 Courage Leagues 1 & 2
  Tennents Regional Leagues
  Heineken Leagues 1 & 2
Sun 31 Glasgow v Edinburgh

JANUARY 1996
Sat 6 Italy v Scotland A
  Italy Under-21 v Scotland Under-21
  Courage Leagues 1 & 2
  Courage Leagues 3 & 4
  Courage Leagues Other Divs
  Tennents Regional Leagues
  Tennents National Leagues 1 to 7
  Heineken Leagues 1 to 5
  Wales Schools v Scotland Schools
Sat 13 Courage Leagues 3 & 4
  Courage Leagues Other Divs
  Tennents Regional Leagues
  Tennents National Leagues 1 to 7
  Heineken Leagues 1 to 5
Fri 19 France A v England A
  France Students v England Students
  Ireland A v Scotland A
  Ireland Under-21 v Scotland Under-21
Sat 20 FRANCE v ENGLAND
  IRELAND v SCOTLAND
  SWALEC Cup 5th Round
Mon 22 Heineken Leagues 5
Sat 27 Pilkington Cup 5th Round
  Pilkington Shield 6th Round
  Tennents Regional Leagues
  Tennents National Leagues 1 to 7
  Heineken Leagues 3 to 5
  Irish Provincial Cups 1st Round

FEBRUARY 1996
Fri 2 England Students v Wales Students
  Scotland A v France A
  Scotland Under-21 v France Under-21
  Wales A v France A
Sat 3 ENGLAND v WALES

  SCOTLAND v FRANCE
  Irish Provincial Cups 2nd Round
Sat 10 Courage Leagues 1 & 2
  Courage Leagues 3 & 4
  Courage Leagues Other Divs
  Tennents National Leagues 1 to 7
  Heineken Leagues 3 to 5
Sun 11 Scotland Students v New South Wales
    Students
Fri 16 Wales A v Scotland A
  Wales Under-21 v Scotland Under-21
  Wales Students v Scotland Students
Sat 17 FRANCE v IRELAND
  WALES v SCOTLAND
  Courage Leagues 1 to 4
  Courage Leagues Other Divs
  Wales Youth v Italian Youth
Sat 24 Pilkington Cup Quarter-finals
  Pilkington Shield Quarter-finals
  Courage Leagues 3 & 4
  Courage Leagues Other Divs
  Tennents 1556 Cup 4th Round
  SWALEC Cup 6th Round
  Wales Youth v Ireland Youth

MARCH 1996
Fri 1 Scotland Students v England Students
  Ireland A v Wales A
  Ireland Under-21 v Wales Under-21
  Ireland Students v Wales Students
Sat 2 IRELAND v WALES
  SCOTLAND v ENGLAND
Wed 6 East Midlands v Barbarians
Sat 9 Italy Colts v England Colts
  CIS County Championship Semi-finals
  Tennents National Leagues 1 to 7
  Heineken Leagues 1 to 5
  French Juniors v Welsh Youth
Fri 15 England A v Ireland A
  England Students v Ireland Students
  Wales Under-21 v France Under-21
  Wales Students v France Students
Sat 16 ENGLAND v IRELAND
  WALES v FRANCE
  Tennents 1556 Cup 5th Round
Sat 20 CIS Insurance County Championship
  CIS Insurance U-21 County Championship

	Heineken Leagues 1 to 5
	Insurance Corporation Leagues 1 to 4
	England Colts v France Colts
	Scotland Under-19 v Wales Under-19
	Scotland Under-18 v Wales Under-18
Sun 21	Tennents 1556 Cup 6th Round
	Insurance Corporation Leagues 2
	Wanderers v Dolphin
Sat 27	Courage Leagues 1 to 4
	Heineken Leagues 1 to 5
	Irish Provincial Cups – Semi-finals
Sun 28	Tennents 1556 Cup 7th Round

APRIL 1996

Sat 6	Cardiff v Barbarians
	Courage Leagues 1 to 4
	Heineken Leagues Divs 1 to 5
	Insurance Corporation Leagues 1 to 4
	France UNSS v England 18
	Ireland Schools v Scotland Schools
Wed 10	Royal Navy v Royal Air Force
	England v Ireland (18 Group)
Sat 13	Courage Leagues 1 to 4
	Swalec Cup Semi-Finals
	Insurance Corporation League 1 to 4
	England Colts v Scotland Colts
	Ireland Under-18 v Scotland Under-18
Wed 16	Army v Royal Air Force
Sat 20	CIS Insurance County Championship
	CIS Insurance U-21 County Championship
	Heineken Leagues Divs 1 to 5
	Insurance Corporation Leagues 1 to 4
	England Colts v France Colts
	Scotland Under-19 v Wales Under-19
	Scotland Under-18 v Wales Under-18
Sun 21	Scottish Tennents 1556 Cup 6th Round
	Insurance Corporation League Div 2
	Wanderers v Dolphin
Sat 27	Courage Leagues 1 to 4
	Heineken Leagues Divs 1 to 5
	Provincial Cups - Semi-finals
Sun 28	Scottish Tennents 1556 Cup 7th Round

MAY 1996

Sat 4	Pilkington Cup Final
	Pilkington Shield Final
	SWALEC Cup Final
Sun 5	Irish Provincial Cups – Finals
	Tennents 1556 Cup Semi-finals
Sat 11	Middlesex Seven-a-Side Finals
	Tennents 1556 Cup Final